HOW TO
BUY
A HOUSE

HOW TO
BUY
A HOUSE

by
Joel Makower

A Tilden Press Book
published by
Perigee Books

Perigee Books
are published by
The Putnam Publishing Group
200 Madison Avenue
New York, NY 10016

Library of Congress Cataloging-in-Publication Data

Makower, Joel, date.
    How to buy a house / by Joel Makower. How to sell a house / by
Joel Makower.
       p.   cm.
    No collective t.p. Title transcribed from individual title pages.
    Two works bound together back-to-back.
    "A Tilden Press book."
    1. House buying.   2. House selling.   I. Makower, Joel, date.
How to sell a house.   1989.   II. Title.   III. Title: How to sell
a house.
    ISBN 0-399-51565-8
    HD1379.M353   1989   89-33668 CIP
    643' . 12—dc20

Printed in the United States of America

1 2 3 4 5 6 7 8 9 10

ACKNOWLEDGMENTS

Thanks to Linda Zaleskie, who provided valuable research
and organization. Thanks especially to Frances Makower,
agent extraordinaire, for her comments on the manuscript.

CONTENTS

Preface

It's the American Dream: owning your own home. And millions of people do just that—about 65 percent of all American households call themselves homeowners. And with few exceptions—such as those who inherited their home or built it themselves—all of them went through the arduous process of finding, evaluating, deciding on, and paying for their new home.

In the pages that follow, we'll go through that process step by step. You'll learn the ins and outs of finding the right house and getting the best deal. You'll learn the secrets of the experts and get some insight into some of the things to look for—and look out for—when shopping for real estate.

This book will deal primarily with buying a house, although much of the information will apply equally to apartments, condominiums, and cooperatives. It assumes that you are buying a house to live in, not for investment purposes, although a great deal of information will be applicable to such purchases as well. (Investment real estate involves additional concerns that are beyond the scope of this book.)

As you'll learn, buying a house requires that you put together a team—most likely an agent, a lawyer, and an accountant, or reasonable substitutes who are able to fulfill those roles—that can protect your interests and ensure that any purchase meets your individual needs. Always keep in mind when reading this book and when consulting other sources on this subject that your best information will come from people working directly in your interest.

Also keep in mind that there are hundreds of laws dealing with real estate transactions—federal, state, and local—and that these laws are subject to change on a regular basis. Of particular concern is the financial aspect of real estate: Loan rates, loan types, and tax angles seem to change with the tides. It will be of vital importance that you or your advisers keep up to date on these matters.

Overall, the important thing to remember when buying a house is that every home, and every individual, is unique. Your success as a buyer will be directly related to your ability to keep your particular needs in mind at all times.

Chapter 1
Why Buy?

Do you really want to buy a house? That may seem like a simplistic question. "Of course I do," you may be saying. "That's why I'm reading this book." Perhaps. But the question remains: Is purchasing a house really in your best interest?

The answer may not be as obvious as you think. While there are a lot of good reasons for buying a place to live, owning real estate is not for everybody. And if you already own a house and are considering moving to another one, there may be far cheaper alternatives. Before you dive head first into the complexities of finding and buying a house, you may first want to see if other options make better sense. You may save yourself a lot of time, trouble, and money in the process.

BUYING VS. RENTING

If you're presently a renter, you should take a hard look at the realities of owning real estate. Among the questions you should ask yourself:

❏ *How do I like to spend my time?* Do you like to putter around and fix things? Do you mind painting, scraping, installing, patching, tightening, and mending? Any home, including the newest, freshly renovated residence, will require a seemingly endless array of to-do's. Of course, if you have more money than time, this won't be a problem: you can hire someone to do it for you. But since this isn't the case for most of us, get ready to spend some of those free weekends and days off working on your house.

❏ *How long do I plan to live here?* If it's only a year or two, you may be better off renting. For one thing, the closing costs—the taxes and other fees you must pay to a wide range of individuals when you buy, sell, and finance real estate—add thousands of dollars to the first-year cost of ownership. To pay those fees every year or two (or three) may not make financial sense. You could be better off renting, although you'll have to figure this out for yourself. Assume that closing costs will equal roughly 5 to 10 percent of the house's purchase price.

❏ *Is this the best thing I can do with my money?* It might be, but it might not. Home ownership comes with some pretty attractive tax deductions, not to mention a convenient way of building investment equity. But depending on your age, income, and other factors, these financial conditions may not be what you need. If you have a modest income and have other tax deductions—children, child care, medical expenses, or business losses, for example—you may not need homeowners' deductions. If you're older, nearing retirement, and have a reasonable nest egg, you may not be concerned with building equity. You may be better off investing your money elsewhere. Again, you should examine your particular situation with a financial professional. You should not count on a real estate agent to provide you with this information.

❏ *How much can I afford to spend on shelter?* It may seem that you're already stretched to the limit every month, so the additional cost of a mortgage compared to rent may not be wise to assume. But keep in mind that with the additional deductions you'll get with your house, you may be able to increase your W-2 deductions, meaning that your employer will withhold less from each paycheck, and you'll have more take-home pay. We'll get into these financial considerations more in Chapter 4.

To assist you in making your rent-vs.-buy decision, it may help to take a hard look at renting. There are several advantages:

❏ Monthly payments are usually lower than when buying.
❏ You needn't make any substantial down payment, other than a security fee and your last month's rent.
❏ You usually don't have to pay for fixing things that break, such as the plumbing, electricity, roof leaks, and other major systems.
❏ If heat or other utilities are included in your rent, you won't have to worry about being hit by fuel increases or the energy costs of a particularly cold winter or hot summer.

❑ When you decide to pick up and move, there is little you need to do other than provide your landlord with thirty days' notice, or whatever other terms are specified in your lease.

In short, there is little financial risk, little commitment to how long you live there, and few worries. However, there *are* some disadvantages to renting, especially when compared to buying:

❑ You won't get any tax breaks for renting.

❑ While most (but not all) monthly mortgage payments stay the same for the life of the loan, your rent can—and will—increase every year or two.

❑ You are at the mercy of your landlord. With luck, this won't be problematic, but not everyone is so lucky. If something goes wrong—your refrigerator breaks, for example, on the weekend—your landlord may not act as quickly as you yourself would if you owned the place. Of course, most states and some cities have laws that require landlords to provide basic necessities (including refrigerators), but the wheels of justice usually don't move a reluctant landlord as quickly as it takes for a freezerful of steaks to defrost.

❑ You'll have nothing to show for your monthly rental payments, other than a fistful of canceled checks. This may seem OK today, but a few years down the road, it may hit you that for a few extra dollars a month, you could be building your future wealth.

ADVANTAGES AND DISADVANTAGES OF BUYING

Now, let's look at the advantages and disadvantages of buying. First, the good news:

❑ Buying real estate is a sound financial investment. Historically, it is an appreciating—or at least stable—asset, meaning that your home's value will probably increase over time, or at least retain its value. In general, owning a home is a good way to beat inflation. But not always: Several factors, including the economy, the local real estate market, and the house itself, could affect a home's value in a negative way. But such conditions represent more the exception than the rule.

❑ The longer you own it, the greater the equity you build,

meaning the more of the house that you actually own.

❏ Homeowners who regularly pay their mortgage on time usually represent the best financial risks, making it easier to get a loan if you ever need one.

❏ There are significant tax advantages to owning. When you file your income tax return, you'll be able to deduct hundreds or thousands of dollars in mortgage interest payments from your income, effectively reducing your monthly mortgage by up to a third. In addition, as a homeowner, you can borrow additional money against your home's value, and deduct *that* interest, too. And you can be sure that no matter how much government officials change the tax structure, this special privilege for homeowners won't be affected much, if at all.

❏ If you buy in a neighborhood in which most of your neighbors are also owners, the neighborhood will probably be cleaner, safer, quieter, and friendlier than a neighborhood made up predominantly of renters.

❏ Perhaps the best reason to buy, psychologically at least, is that owning offers you certain freedoms you won't have as a renter, including increased privacy and the ability to live the way you want.

Of course, there are some disadvantages:

❏ You'll generally need a chunk of cash to buy a house—at least 5 percent of the purchase price, and possibly as much as 20 percent.

❏ Real estate is a nonliquid investment, meaning that if you need the cash you "invested" in buying a house, you won't be able to get it easily, although you probably can borrow money against your home's value.

❏ You've probably heard the expression "house poor." A house can be a severe financial drain, from both expected (homeowners insurance, local taxes, and utilities) and unexpected (emergency repairs or property-tax increases) expenses.

❏ As stated earlier, a house can be a lot of work, from mowing the lawn to fixing leaky pipes to taking care of a hundred trivial and not-so-trivial matters. And the longer you put off making these needed repairs, the worse they'll get.

❏ You can't move quite as quickly from a home you own as from one you're renting. As you'll learn in later chapters, the process is indeed time-consuming. Depending on a number of factors, a house can take from two to nine months or more to market, negotiate, sell, and ultimately transfer title.

❏ If you run into financial straits—including health problems, divorce, unemployment—you may not be able to keep up your monthly mortgage payments. If you default on those payments, you could lose your house, along with all the money you've invested in it.

As you can see, a lot of the arguments for buying are financial. And with good reason: Today, probably more than ever before, a house is no longer just a home. It's one of the most important investment decisions you'll ever make. Which is not to say that you'll strike it rich. But over the past twenty years, housing costs have appreciated at the inflation rate plus about three percentage points annually; most experts say that while housing costs are leveling off in most areas, they will still tend to keep up with inflation, and then some. If you look at the numbers, they can be impressive indeed. A study by Chicago Title & Trust Company figured that a house purchased for $133,400 in 1987 would be worth $549,100 in the year 2015, assuming it kept up with an annual 5 percent rate of inflation. If prices were to increase by the same average as over the past decade—8.1 percent—that same $133,400 house would be worth well over $1,000,000 in 2015!

Where you live is one contributing factor to house appreciation. A study by the Census Bureau of twenty-one metropolitan areas found that between 1970 and 1981, home prices appreciated by about 150 percent in the Detroit area (from an average of $19,600 to $48,900) while in the Anaheim, California, area they went up by more than 400 percent (from $27,300 to $137,200).

Of course, there are no guarantees that the house you buy will appreciate in value, and you shouldn't count on any of these figures. The point is that, historically, owning a house has been an extremely good investment.

In the end, however, whether or not you buy is a personal decision that has as much to do with dreams and desire as reality. Having considered the above, you may determine that your financial situation doesn't really justify buying, but the pleasure you'd get out of being your own landlord would more than make up for the financial struggles. If so—and you're not dissuaded from your dream by bankers, accountants, real estate agents, and the like—you are encouraged to follow your dream. On the other hand, if money is not the issue, but you're not up to the hassles of owning—and you can find something better to do with your money—you may want to hold off.

FIXING UP YOUR PRESENT HOME

If you are presently a homeowner, and are considering seeking another house that better suits your present needs, consider this: You may be better off fixing up, adding to, or otherwise altering your present house instead. According to a survey conducted by the National Association of Home Builders, the two major reasons homeowners seek another home are for better energy efficiency and more space.

There are countless ways to conserve energy: new windows and doors, weatherstripping and caulking, better insulation, new energy-efficient appliances, a new heating system, solar energy panels, and a host of other improvements. You owe it to yourself to look into any of a variety of books on the subject of saving energy and "retrofitting" your existing home in energy-saving ways. The money you'd invest in energy savings will likely pay itself back over time, or will improve the value of your house when you finally do decide to sell it. Moreover, if you need to borrow money to make these improvements, you'll be able to deduct the interest you pay on the loan on your taxes.

Somewhat more ambitious, but even more rewarding, is to repair or remodel your present house to better suit your needs. After all, instead of searching and searching for a new house—which still probably won't exactly fit your ideal—why not take the place you now call home and *make* it fit your needs? You'll endure some discomfort, to be sure, but probably less than packing up, moving to a new house, and settling in a new neighborhood.

Start by making a wish list. Let your fantasies run wild: Another bedroom or two. An extra bathroom. The existing bathrooms remodeled. A new and bigger kitchen. A master bedroom suite. A new family room. A deck. A swimming pool. A hot tub. A new paint job inside and out. It may be that these things just aren't practical; your house has no room to grow, for example, or you'd rather simply start from scratch at a new location. And you may want to move to a specific new neighborhood or region.

But you might be surprised. By investing in your existing home, you'll do more than make it a more comfortable place to live, you'll have increased its value and thereby benefit when you decide to sell it. And you may do all this for less than the cost of moving and buying a new place. It's probably worth spending some time talking to a contractor (most will give you a reasonable estimate at no charge) and to an accountant or other financial counselor about this choice.

AN IMPOSSIBLE DREAM?

To a great many would-be home buyers—particularly first-time buyers—the prospect of purchasing a house seems distant, if not impossible. Prices in many areas are skyrocketing. In some cities, it is virtually impossible to find a decent home in a reasonable neighborhood for under $150,000. And the stories you read in the paper and hear on the news don't help much: They dwell on how high the cost of housing is going, and on how many fewer people seem able to afford a home compared to a decade ago.

But keep this mind: These reports are based on statistics for an entire city or state. It doesn't consider your individual situation. You need to buy only one house. Thousands of people do it every week, and the overwhelming majority are extremely happy with their purchase. It may take some time, it may take some mirrors and string and creative financing, but it can be done. And the longer you try, the more likely it is that you'll succeed.

Chapter 2
Setting Your Sights

Consider your home search to be something of a well-orchestrated battle plan. Your chances of victory are directly linked to how well you prepare and execute that plan. You needn't make this a formal battle plan with forms, charts, maps, and diagrams; indeed, much of it needn't even be written down. But the more you prepare, the better off you'll be.

In the most general sense, the first two steps in your battle plan will look something like this:

❏ **Step One:** Evaluating your housing needs
❏ **Step Two:** Figuring out what you can actually afford

Let's take it a step at a time.

Step One: How and Where Do You Want to Live?

Let's overlook your initial answer to this question—it's probably "Like a king (or queen) . . . in a castle . . . on an island." We need to get a bit more realistic. Now is the time to set forth some basic needs you'll have. These can change later on, after you've taken a closer look at the local real estate market. But at least it gives you some place to start. Your goal here is to define as closely as possible what kind of accommodation will best suit the way you live.

Among the things to think about are:

❏ *Location.* Do you need to be close to your work? Are you willing to commute? How long—a half hour? An hour? More? How about city vs. suburbs vs. country? Are there specific parts of a city that you find appealing—close to the major park; near a lot of restaurants you can walk to; near the best elementary school; far from the local college? Do you need to "get away from it all" when you come home from work? Is location even important? Would you be willing to live just about anywhere within reason, if it meant getting the right house? One obvious factor here is whether you have—or are planning to have—children. If so, you probably have some ideas about the kind of neighborhood or area in which you'd like them to grow up.

How about public transportation? If you're older, or if you have children who need to take buses to school or other activities, this may be an important factor. How about any of the following—is it important for you to live near one or more of these?

✔ Department stores
✔ Hospitals
✔ Parks
✔ Restaurants
✔ Schools
✔ Supermarkets
✔ Theaters

If you have some neighborhoods or towns in mind, you should pay them a visit—not just once, but several times. And don't just drive through them. Get out of the car and walk around. Go into the local supermarket, eat at a local restaurant, check out a local drugstore, walk down Main Street. You'll begin to get a feel for whether this location is really a good choice.

Some basic research may be needed. If, for example, you are moving to a new town or city, you may not be familiar with the local school system. And looks may be deceiving: The shiniest new suburb may have the most underfunded school system compared with the older, more established one closer to downtown. On the other hand, a lavish public school system may indicate that local real estate taxes are sky high. Moving to the next suburb or town could make a difference of hundreds or thousands of dollars in taxes alone.

More about location later on in this chapter. Again, your choice of location is not set in stone. It's just a beginning, a place to start looking.

❑ *Space.* How much space do you need? How many bedrooms, bathrooms, and other rooms (dining room, recreation room, laundry room, den, attic, basement, garage)? And consider the area outside the house: Do you need a backyard? Will it be used for flowers, children, pets, boats, a pool, or some combination thereof?

Consider carefully your personal situation and lifestyle. Are you newly married or single? Will your family be growing in the foreseeable future? Do you entertain much? Do you regularly have visitors coming in from out of town? Are there hobbies that need a special space (darkroom, workshop, sewing room)? Do you tend to keep a lot of possessions in storage? If so, you may want a room solely for this purpose.

This is something you probably should commit to paper. Make a "wish list"— a reasonable one, unless you don't anticipate money being a factor in your purchase decision. Place an asterisk next to those items you can definitely live without, perhaps ranking them in importance. For example:

✔ master bedroom
✔ two children's bedrooms
✔ guest bedroom* (1)
✔ master bathroom
✔ children's bathroom
✔ half bathroom downstairs* (3)
✔ living room
✔ dining room
✔ family room* (4)
✔ den/office
✔ laundry room
✔ basement/storage room
✔ sewing room* (2)
✔ two-car garage
✔ backyard with swing set* (5)

Be as specific as possible. If you can specify the sizes of the rooms you'd prefer, that will be helpful when it comes to actually inspecting prospective properties. If, for example, you know your present (12' x 14') bedroom is definitely too small, you should note that down, perhaps specifying the ideal size. Chances are, whether you now rent or own, you know what's lacking in your present home. These should be considered and noted on your wish list. As you look at houses (don't forget your trusty tape measure), you can compare each property to your specifications. Without this list, you may overlook some things important to you.

Think about your special needs. Will stairs— either those leading up to your front door or those going to the upstairs rooms— cause difficulty for anyone, either now or in the next few years? Do you have a pet that tends to track in dirt and mud that might require back-door access leading into a "mud room"?

Also important to consider is how much land you'd like to have. Forget about the fact that most of us want our own little acre on a hilltop— or, in some people's case, an emerald forest in an enchanted land. We're talking reality here, or some reasonable facsimile thereof. Do you want a backyard big enough to exercise your golden retriever and accommodate a full swing set for your kids *and* a putting green for yourself? Do you need a backyard at all? (To some people, a backyard means only one thing: endless weeding.)

We'll worry later about whether or not you can afford all this.

❏ *Special Features.* Our wish list-making is only starting. Now that you've decided on the number of rooms in your ideal house, it's time to get specific about amenities. Rank the items in order of importance. For example:

✔ wood-burning fireplace
✔ central air conditioning
✔ eat-in kitchen
✔ dishwasher
✔ gas stove
✔ deadbolt locks
✔ garbage disposal
✔ wall-to-wall carpeting
✔ walk-in pantry
✔ skylights
✔ ceiling fans
✔ walk-in closets
✔ screened porch

Again, we're talking about an ideal here. Real costs will be discussed next.

STEP TWO: WHAT CAN YOU REALLY AFFORD?

If you've read or heard anything about home buying in the past few years, you may have come across the term "affordability gap." The term refers to the difference between the rate of increase in housing costs and the rate of increase in incomes. To hear some of the reports, you'd think no one could afford to buy a home today. And yet people buy houses every day! True, they may not all get the houses of their dreams, but they do manage to buy a house, and somehow manage to make them affordable.

To understand the subject of affordability of houses, it will help first to understand how real estate is financed, and how lenders make decisions about how much they may be willing to lend you, assuming certain other factors.

There are several methods for determining how much of a mortgage you can take on:

❑ *The Multiplier Method.* This is a rule of thumb that says that lenders consider you are reasonably able to carry a mortgage equal to *between 1.5 and 3 times your gross annual income*. The exact multiplier depends largely on current interest rates. When they are low— say, under 12 percent— lenders use the one-and-a-half multiplier. As interest rates rise, so does the multiplier. So, if your annual income is $50,000, you could reasonably afford to pay a mortgage of between $75,000 and $150,000, depending on current conditions.

Now, keep in mind that the mortgage doesn't necessarily equal the price of the house. In fact, you will need to shell out at least 5 percent of the purchase price as the down payment, although the amount could be as much as 20 percent. So, if you buy a $100,000 house and put down 10 percent ($10,000), you will need a $90,000 mortgage. (There are ways of lowering the mortgage and increasing your down payment, which we'll get into in Chapter 4.)

Another multiplier says that you can reasonably afford to pay *between 2 and 2.5 times your annual take-home pay*— that is, your gross pay less federal, state, local, and social security taxes. So, if your annual take-home pay equals $38,000, you could be expected to carry a mortgage of between $76,000 and $95,000.

Rules of thumb are tricky, because they assume that you are "average," which, of course, nobody is. Your particular circumstances will be determined by your other monthly payments for items such as credit card purchases, other loans, tuition, and alimony. They also will be affected by how much money you put down (the less you put down, the more you'll need to borrow), whether you are buying a new or older house (older houses often require regular infusions of cash for repairs), and by the stability of your income. Your particular circumstances also depend on the part of the country in which you are buying.

❏ *The Percentage Method.* This says that a family should devote *no more than 28 percent of its income to housing costs*, including the mortgage, insurance, and real estate taxes. And if you have other long-term debts, such as a car loan or tuition, the cost of those loans plus your housing costs shouldn't exceed 36 percent. However, if you're making a down payment of only 10 percent, some lenders won't allow you to put more than 25 percent of your gross income into housing costs, or 33 percent of your total monthly debt payments.

Remember that these percentages include all housing costs. In addition to mortgage, insurance, and taxes, some lenders also include maintenance, utilities, and other costs in their calculations.

❏ *The Itemization Method.* The most accurate way to determine how much you can probably borrow is to do exactly what you'll have to do eventually when you come face to face with a potential lender: itemize your exact monthly income and expenses. To do this, you need to devise a simple budget worksheet with two columns— one for assets and income, the other for liabilities and expenses. A sample worksheet is included on the next page

The way this method works is that you'll—

SAMPLE HOUSING COST WORKSHEET

A. Your monthly income

Take-home pay	$ _____
Other monthly income (rents, dividends, interest)	_____
Other reliable income sources (list):	
_____	_____
_____	_____
_____	_____

TOTAL MONTHLY INCOME (1) $ _____

B. Your monthly non-housing expenses

Food, household items	$ _____
Clothing	_____
Medical costs and insurance	_____
Life insurance	_____
Other insurance	_____
Telephone	_____
Interest payments	_____
Entertainment	_____
Other personal expenses	_____
Commuting	_____
Education	_____
Savings	_____
Other (list):	
_____	_____
_____	_____
_____	_____

TOTAL MONTHLY EXPENSES (2) $ _____

C. Money Available for Housing

Total Monthly Income (1)	$ _____
[less Total Monthly Expenses (2)]	_____

MONTHLY INCOME FOR HOUSING $ _____

1. start with your monthly take-home pay;
2. subtract your monthly expenses; and
3. end up with the amount of money you'll have available for owning a house.

As a guide, figure that about two-thirds of the money available for housing will go toward mortgage payments. The balance will go toward the other items mentioned above— insurance, taxes, and all the other costs of maintenance and repair, utilities, and so forth.

Now, keep in mind that all three of these methods are only rough guides. The actual amount you'll be able to borrow will be determined, of course, by the lender.

❑ *Closing Costs.* Your mortgage isn't the only factor to consider. When you buy a house, there is a host of other "closing" costs— fees and taxes that must be paid at the time the property changes hands. These costs include lawyers' fees, appraisal fees, title search fees, and payment of property taxes, among others. All told, closing costs typically run between 5 and 10 percent of the amount of the mortgage. Assuming a $75,000 mortgage, that's equal to between $3,750 and $7,500. It's a relatively modest amount, but remember: This is *not* an amount that you can finance over thirty years, like the house itself. You must pay closing costs up front, in cash.

❑ *Moving Expenses.* This is an often overlooked cost of buying a house. Your budget should include such things as deposits for utility and phone companies, moving companies, and other necessities your new home will require immediately.

OLD HOUSES VS. NEW HOUSES
One key issue is whether you prefer to buy a newly built home or an older, existing home. Some people like older homes. They have character, they tend to be in established neighborhoods, they may even come with a bit of history. Others prefer spanking new models, with completely modern fixtures and appliances, often more energy efficient, sometimes with more space and a bigger yard, albeit probably an unlandscaped one. A "new"

home, in the world of real estate, can refer to any residence that's under five years old.

Buying an existing home has some of the same risks as buying a used car: You won't know *exactly* what's wrong with it. You can get a pretty good idea, though, by hiring a professional home inspector (more about that in Chapter 3), but even he or she won't give you any guarantees. In general, however, older homes are better built than newer ones, often constructed with greater stress loads and more soundproof walls than newer homes. Another good thing about existing homes is that there are more of them on the market at any given moment— about fifty times more than newer homes, according to one estimate.

New homes, like new cars, aren't immune to problems either. Indeed, there can be "lemons"— houses that have so many little (and not-so-little) problems that things never seem to get completely right. Like cars, many new homes come with extended warranties— one of the most common is HOW, Home Owners Warranty— that can provide protection against major structural defects for up to ten years. Such warranties are offered by the home builder at the time of settlement. You can get more information on HOW by writing to Home Owners Warranty Corporation, 2000 L Street NW, Washington, DC 20036.

There are warranties available for older homes, too. The National Association of Realtors offers its members a warranty program. Some plans require a property inspection by an independent inspector, and coverage is limited to those items inspected and approved. Plans generally cover major operating systems, such as heating, plumbing, electrical, and air conditioning, as well as the structural soundness of the exterior and interior walls, ceilings, and floor.

One of the biggest problems with new homes is getting them finished. Often, new homes are purchased based on a model home not unlike the one you'll actually buy. But getting your actual home built can take months longer than planned, which may put a definite kink in your plans. You may be allowed to move in before your house is truly finished, but those last few touches can take an agonizingly long time to be completed. And after all that, your house might not even closely resemble the model you'd based your purchase on.

There are other advantages and disadvantages to buying new and older homes. *New homes* tend to have finished basements, more insulation, more energy efficient heating and cooling systems, are farther from center cities, have more closet space, and generally are in lower-crime areas. On the other hand, those in brand new developments may not be close to transportation and may look like all the other houses in the same development. *Older homes* tend to be nearer shopping areas and public transportation, and generally have better public services, including police, fire, and mail service. On the other hand, you are more likely to have to replace appliances, add insulation, replace windows, and upgrade other components or systems.

Ultimately, your old-versus-new decision will probably be determined by personal preference, location, and price.

LOCATION, LOCATION, LOCATION

When you purchase a house, you're buying more than just the property. You're also "buying" a neighborhood and, along with that, neighbors. While there are a great many people who exist quite comfortably in neighborhoods in they may not necessarily like, it is a great advantage to find a place that will appeal to you. If it does appeal to you, it likely will appeal to others, meaning that the value of the property will probably be stable, or possibly increase substantially through the years. Simply put, buying in a good neighborhood is like buying a blue-chip stock.

But what makes a "good" neighborhood? Unfortunately, there's no one firm answer, and no easy way to find out what constitutes such a neighborhood. But you can learn a lot just by walking around an area, using your five senses, and asking questions of people in the area that interests you.

In doing your research, you'll want to know not just what the neighborhood is like now, but where it is going. The neighborhood's future will have an effect on the value of a home and your ability to sell it later on. It will take more than just looking around to determine this. Some neighborhoods may look all right, but after asking some questions you may find it's going downhill. One indication would be a lot of vacant houses or for sale signs. It could mean that a growing number of people are frustrated with the noise, litter, crime, or whatever. Similarly, a neighborhood that doesn't look great may not necessarily be a "bad" neighborhood.

Schools are one place to find the answer, even if you don't have school-age children. The quality of local schools can tell you a lot about a neighborhood. According to Anthony B. Sanders, a professor of real estate finance at Ohio State University, positive trends in the scholastic rankings of a school district indicate a neighborhood on the way up. Crime rates are another obvious indicator. A visit to the local police precinct headquarters or a chat with a police officer on the street could tell you all you need to know about the local crime scene.

Owner occupancy is still another indicator of value. Neighborhoods where there are more owners than renters tend to be more stable and better taken care of. If there are a lot of recent renters, it could mean that unfavorable conditions resulted in owners leaving the neighborhoods, renting out their homes to others. That's not a good sign.

If you really want to do some digging, consider going to a local library and looking through one- or two-year-old real estate classified ads for the same neighborhoods you are considering. If home prices seem to be rising faster than those in the rest of the region, it's a good bet that they will continue to rise— and that the neighborhood will continue to improve. Another good source of information is the local land use or planning office. Officials there can provide some insight about a neighborhood, and perhaps tell you about any future development that may affect home values.

Timing, of course, is of the essence, particularly when considering neighborhoods that may be "marginal," to use a common euphemism. You may find an improving neighborhood, but it may take a year or so before it rises to the level that you find acceptable. But if you find the right neighborhood too late, you may be priced out of the market.

❏ *Evaluating a neighborhood.* Everyone has different needs for their neighborhood. Here are some things to think about:

✔ Are the homes well taken care of?

✔ Is the neighborhood pleasant to look at?

✔ Is it convenient to shops, places of worship, theaters, and recreational facilities?

✔ Is it close enough to (or far enough from) where you work?

✔ Is there adequate street parking?

✔ What are the commuting conditions like?

✔ Is it accessible to public transportation?

✔ If you have children, will there be other children nearby to play with?

✔ Is there any history of flooding during storms?

✔ Are there any nearby vacant lots or abandoned buildings that are ripe for development?

✔ Are there nearby factories, interstates, or other potential sources of noise or pollution?

✔ Is there decent radio and TV reception?

Zoning may be a factor if you plan to add on to your home. Additions that affect the outside of your house— a deck, porch, fence, or satellite dish, for instance— may require permission or may be banned altogether. You may be subject to zoning regulations if you have a pet, boat, or recreational vehicle. And zoning may also be a factor if you plan to rent out part of the house or adjacent property.

WHAT CONSTITUTES VALUE?

Value. We hear the word all the time— in supermarkets, department stores, car showrooms, anywhere that things are being sold. And we all want it; "value" means we are getting the most for our money. Clearly, when shopping for the biggest purchase of all, you'll want to make sure you get the most value possible. Moreover, with real estate, value has an additional meaning: A home with value is most likely to appreciate at or above the prevailing real estate market rates.

What comprises value in a home? Before you begin looking at specific properties, you should consider what others find valuable in a home. According to the National Association of Home Builders, here are the ten most valued things people consider when buying a *new* home:

❏ Quality workmanship
❏ Neighborhood
❏ Builder reputation
❏ Energy features
❏ Warranty
❏ Exterior appearance
❏ Location to shopping
❏ School district
❏ Location to work
❏ Security alarm systems

A similar list for existing homes would probably look a bit different, although most items would appear somewhere on the list. Energy efficiency would probably rank high; exterior appearance might rank lower. But room configuration—the number and sizes of rooms—would likely be a key consideration of value. (This isn't as much of a concern with new homes, because almost any new home will have at least three bedrooms and two baths, something you can't assume for an existing home.) Three- and four-bedroom houses are generally considered the best investments, provided they have at least two full baths. Also valuable in existing homes is the ability to add on rooms—building either up, down, or out—that could turn a less than desirable residence into a hot property.

Of course, your list of priorities may not resemble these at all. Closeness to work may be foremost among your considerations, for example, and a few large rooms may be more appealing than many smaller ones.

You should also be aware of what *doesn't* comprise value. Sellers of both new and existing homes are prone to highlight any of dozens of factors that aren't really that important, but that may *sound* important if the seller presents them in an important fashion. A good paint job, for example, while desirable, isn't that valuable, because you could always have one done (or do it yourself) for a thousand dollars or so. The same with wall-to-wall carpeting; chances are that unless the carpeting is in top-notch shape and perfectly fits your decor, you'll be replacing it within a few years anyway. So, too, with light fixtures, fancy wallpaper, even basic landscaping—in other words, those things not part of intrinsically valuable things such as the home's location and structure. Admittedly, this can get somewhat arbitrary. Some things—like well-preserved hardwood floors, extra built-in appliances, or double-wall construction— might or might not be of value to you. It always comes down to a matter of personal need and preference.

HOW SELLERS DETERMINE VALUE

Ultimately, aside whatever you determine as valuable in a home, you also have to understand the seller's determination of value. When the asking price of a home is set— by the real estate agent, the owner, or whomever— it isn't easy to anticipate the personal preferences of those who will be looking at it. So their determination will be much more hard-nosed, based on fact and figures— and a touch of gut feeling. Professional real estate agents use some or all of the following to determine the value of a property:

❑ The recent actual selling prices of nearby properties.
❑ The home's condition.
❑ The home's replacement cost.
❑ The seller's motivation.
❑ Their own personal taste.

As you can see, setting home prices is equal parts art and science. This knowledge will be helpful later on as you look at prospective properties.

THE RIGHT TIME TO BUY

Is there a "right" time to buy a house? Yes and no. While there are certain conditions—personal conditions and market conditions— that turn home buying to your advantage, we don't always have the luxury of choosing the best time to purchase a home. Job relocation, divorce, or the death of a spouse may impose an unwanted time frame on you. But if the matter of timing is your own choice, here are some things to think about.

Is it the right time for you? This is really a financial question, one that may require assistance from an accountant, financial planner, investment adviser, or other guru. Some questions to ask:

❑ *Do you have, or can you get, enough cash?* As outlined earlier, you'll need money for the down payment, closing costs, move-in costs, and probably some immediate fix-up costs.

❑ *Is your job and family situation stable?* Is there a steady, reliable source of income? Are your marital or other living arrangements intact? Changes in your job or family (including births, deaths, and health problems) can make it harder for you to pay for the house.

❑ *Is your credit good?* As you can imagine, your good credit will go a long way toward getting the mortgage you need. If it's not good, consider taking some steps to get it in better shape. There are many such steps; consult a banker or nonprofit consumer credit counseling service for details.

Is it a buyer's or seller's market? This can have a big impact on the price you pay for a house. A buyer's market exists when there are considerably more available homes than buyers. Because buyers have the luxury of picking and choosing, sellers won't be able to command top dollar for their properties. A seller's market, in contrast, exists when there are considerably more buyers than available homes. Buyers can't be as choosy, so sellers are able to charge top dollar.

Another factor in creating a buyer's or seller's market is interest rates. When money is "loose"— that is, when rates are low and lenders are making it readily available with fewer restrictions—prospective buyers tend to go house shopping. Coupled with a shortage of desirable housing, that would create a seller's market. On the other hand, if money is "tight"— rates are high, and lenders are being more restrictive on the kinds of properties for which they'll give mortgages— there will be fewer buyers going house shopping, helping to create a buyer's market. Of course, there are other combinations—loose money and a glut of available homes, or tight money and a paucity of available homes— that tend to cancel each other out, making the market more or less equal.

So, simply put, the best time to buy a house is when

everyone else is selling. The strongest demand for homes usually is in spring and fall, when the weather is nicest and people aren't preoccupied with going to the beach or the mountains. That's when competition for homes is likely to be greatest. If you can buy in between those two seasons— ideally, in July and August, or during the dead of winter—you'll likely be in the best negotiating position.

Conventional wisdom is that the best time to buy a car is the last Saturday in February, particularly if it's snowing, preferably between 3 and 6 P.M. Chances are the showroom will be empty and salespeople will be anxious to meet their monthly quotas. Home sellers generally don't have monthly quotas (more precisely, they have a quota of exactly one house: theirs), but you get the picture. Inclement weather is one great time to go house-hunting, or after a heavy snow or scorching heat wave, when sellers are sitting lonely in their open houses, waiting anxiously for *somebody* to come by and take a look. If you have the luxury of waiting, you're best off finding these times when people who are selling homes can't find buyers. You'll find buyers much more willing to wheel and deal, a subject we'll get to in Chapter 5.

So, having made up your mind to go for it, it's time to start looking for a house to buy.

Chapter 3
A Good House Is
Hard to Find

There's one school of thought that says "Don't make a purchase until you've inspected at least 100 homes in the area in which you're considering buying." That may seem like a pretty tall order; there may not even *be* 100 homes for sale in the area that are worthy of inspection. But the advice makes a good point: The more houses you inspect, the better able you'll be to pick one of them.

What we're talking about here is making a part-time career of looking at available homes. (Indeed, there are a lot of people who get pleasure from doing this, even if they're not in the market for a home. Some of these people simply like to see how other people live.) We're talking about spending most of your weekends driving around and looking—really looking—at homes. Ideally you should look at homes that are above your price range, and homes that are less expensive; homes that are bigger than what you want, and those that are smaller; homes in the best neighborhoods, and those in the less desirable locations.

In the process, you'll gain some valuable experience and information. First and foremost, you'll get a good idea of the possibilities— how much the local real estate market jibes with your housing needs and personal financial realities. You'll also develop a sharper eye for detail: You'll likely see some properties that are in good shape, well taken care of, with lots of attractive features, and some properties that are clearly inferior in terms of their condition, location, size, or other features. Moreover, as you travel around inspecting homes, you'll meet a lot of real estate agents who may know of other homes in the area that may better suit your needs or pocketbook.

You should ideally begin this exercise as early in your home-buying plan as possible, even if you're not thinking of buying for six months. You simply cannot learn too much about the homes in a prospective purchasing area.

USING AN AGENT

One of the most important choices you'll make early on is the decision about whether or not to use a real estate agent. You aren't technically required to use an agent to buy a house— you could deal directly with the seller, perhaps using an attorney for advice, but such cases are rare. And going without an agent means that you'll have to find properties on your own, through the classified and other means, and you may miss some perfectly good properties on the market. Nationally, nine out of ten residential real estate transactions involve at least one agent.

A good agent can be a valuable ally in your search for the right house, but there are some things you must understand. (These individuals are referred as "brokers" and "Realtors"— the latter name refers to those who belong to the National Association of Realtors. In this book, we'll use the term "agent" to refer to all such real estate professionals.)

The first and most important thing to know is that in most cases, a real estate agent represents the *seller* of the property. This simple fact is not understood by a great many home buyers, usually because agents generally don't reveal this. A study by the Federal Trade Commission found that three-fourths of prospective home buyers mistakenly believed that the agent who was driving them around to see houses was representing *their* interests. That's simply not the case: He or she is representing the interests of the owners of the homes you're being shown. Some states are passing laws to make agents reveal this fact— usually in writing—but in most states such disclosure is still only up to the agent and it is up to the client—you—to beware.

Why is this so important to know? Because agents make their living earning commissions from the sales that they make. So, the higher the sales price, the bigger the commission the agent receives. To ask "your" agent to help you negotiate a lower price for buying a house is asking him or her to make less money on the deal. (Later on, we'll talk about the advantages of having a "buyer's broker" when you get serious about a particular property.)

Now that you know this, keep in mind anway that a good real estate agent can give you a lot of information and assistance. An experienced agent will know the local market thoroughly, not only which homes will best suit your interests but also which are overpriced and which are true bargains. An agent who subscribes to the Multiple Listing Service will have a record of all homes listed by all agents in a given area, and will have detailed information about each, sometimes including a photograph of the property. The best part is that agents' services are free; they don't get paid until they make a sale, and even then they are paid by the seller of the property, not the buyer.

FINDING AN AGENT

How do you find a good real estate agent? Like finding any other service providers—from house cleaners to plumbers to dentists—it involves a combination of research and word of mouth.

The best referrals always come from satisfied customers. So, you should start by talking to friends, neighbors, relatives— and friends of friends, neighbors, and relatives—who may recently have bought or sold a home in the area in which you'll be buying. What kind of service did they receive? Would they work with them again? You might also seek referrals from local lenders or a local attorney. If you're being transferred by your company, your company may be able to help in your search. Still another approach is to drive through a neighborhood, looking for SOLD signs. Those indicate a successful transaction, something you too are interested in. You might inquire as to who listed the property, and if any other agent was involved with the sale. As suggested earlier, you might also find potential agents by attending open houses. If you decide to "drop in" to see an agent you know nothing about, at least choose one located as close as possible to where you want to buy.

An agent's qualifications are important but you also want to find someone you like. After all, you may spend more than a few weekends driving around with this individual, looking at potential properties. And you want to find someone who readily understands your needs, and will go out of his or her way to find the right property for you. Keep in mind that if successful this individual will earn several thousand dollars for the work, so you're not necessarily taking advantage of an agent simply because you don't like the first half-dozen properties you're shown.

Here are some of the questions you might ask:

❑ Are you licensed? For how long?
❑ Are you a full- or part-time agent?
❑ Do you belong to a local, state, or national real estate association?
❑ Does your firm participate in a multiple listing service?
❑ How many sales have you closed in the last three months?
❑ Can you help me find financing?
❑ How long have you worked as an agent in the area?

The answer to that last question— about the agent's knowledge of the neighborhood— is key. An agent who has worked in— and, preferably, lived in— the neighborhood in which you are looking will have firsthand knowledge of shopping, schools, places of worship, building codes, tax rates, medical services, city services, crime rates, transportation, and perhaps even your potential neighbors.

It wouldn't hurt to interview more than one agent. But in the end, you'll want to pick only one. There's one erroneous school of thought that says that the more agents you have showing you properties, the better your chances of finding one you like. That simply isn't true. Most agents within a given area can show you all the available properties in a given area. You'll get far better attention when you're the exclusive client of one agent who understands your needs.

When you find an agent you're comfortable with, describe as fully as possible what you're looking for, based on the things you determined in Chapter 2. The agent will ask specific questions about your desires and needs, your financial resources, and your projected timetable. Answer these questions as completely as possible; the more your agent knows, the better he or she will be able to help you. One of the questions will be about financing: How will you pay for the house? The agent will likely start you on the process of applying for a mortgage in order to expedite your purchase once you've found the right place.

FOR SALE BY OWNER

Somewhere between 10 and 15 percent of today's homeowners choose to sell their homes themselves, not through a real estate agent. That means that the agent you hire probably won't show you those properties, because their owners probably aren't paying an agent's commission. Which is to say that even if you use an agent, you'll never see about one out of every nine or ten houses on the market.

There are some advantages for sellers to go without a broker (such deals are often referred to as FSBO— pronounced *FIZZ-bo*— which stands for "For Sale By Owner"), as well as some risks. The major advantage for the seller is avoiding having to pay a commission— typically 6 percent to 8 percent of the sales price. Theoretically, that savings should be passed along to the buyer, although this isn't always the case. As you can imagine, those individuals selling without professional help can vary widely in their knowledge and skills. Some may underprice their properties; others may ask well over their property's market value, based on anything from emotional attachment to greed. And amateurs can lack vital information about their homes.

Which is not to say that you shouldn't consider FSBO properties. Many attractive, well-priced homes are sold directly by their owners. And there are bargains to be had, particularly considering the fact that, according to some estimates, the majority of owners attempting to sell their properties themselves fail to reach a successful closing. As a result, you may be lucky enough to come across a frustrated FSBO seller just before he or she is ready to give up and willing to accept an offer well below the original asking price. But don't even considering going FSBO unless you use the services of an attorney or other real estate professional who can represent your interests and ensure that the deal is transacted in the proper manner. As you'll see later on, ownership laws can be complex, and if done improperly, your deal could get stuck in a legal mess costing you far more money than you may have saved. Ideally, you may want to have your lawyer negotiate on your behalf. Homeowners tend to be very subjective and rather emotional about the value of their property, and a dispassionate lawyer may be able to get through to the objective, rational perspective needed for negotiations.

READING THE ADS

The first thing most people do when they begin their search for a house is to read the ads. In fact, many people start reading their newspaper's classifieds long before they seek an agent. And with good reason: A regular perusal of the ads can give you a good sense of the selling prices of homes in various neighborhoods and communities, and may provide some indication of how quickly (or slowly) homes in your area are selling. Moreover, after a while you'll start to see some patterns, particularly when it comes to noting which agents are offering homes in a particular area; this may be helpful when choosing an agent or agency.

One of the first things you'll notice is the unbelievable number of abbreviations used in the ads, some of which may not be readily decipherable. Here are some of the more common ones:

A/C	air conditioning
ac	acre
appl	appliances
assum	assumable mortgage
BA	bathroom
bal	balcony
blt	built-in
BR	bedroom
brk	brick
bsmt	basement
bth	bath
burg/fire	burglar/fire alarm
CAC	central air conditioning
con	convenient to
ctr	center
dbl	double
DR	dining room
dk	deck
EIK or eat-in	eat-in kitchen
fam rm	family room
FHA	qualifies for FHA financing
fin	finished
flr	floor
fml	formal

fpl	fireplace
gar	garage
gas	gas heating
ingrnd	in-ground pool
in-law	separate apartment
lib	library
lg	large
lndry	laundry room
loc	location
LR	living room
md's	maid's room
mint	excellent condition
mod	modern
mstr	master bedroom
mtg	mortgage
nr	near
occup	occupancy
pnld	paneled
pfl of	professional office
pkg	parking
pvt	private
rec rm	recreation room
rm	room
schls	schools
scpd	landscaped
semi-det	semi-detached
sep ent	separate entrance
shwr	shower
sld dr	sliding doors
spklr	underground sprinkler system
starter	small first home
steam	steam heating
terr	terrace
TH	townhouse
txs	taxes
VA	qualifies for VA financing
WW cpt	wall-to-wall carpeting
wbf	wood-burning fireplace
xtr	extras
yd	yard
yr	year

All that's just for starters. Besides these sometimes awkward abbreviations, you'll be faced with an endless list of glowing phrases that range from the sublime to the ridiculous. Here are just a few examples, and what they *really* mean:

❑ Affordably priced ("The price is fair.")
❑ City chic ("It's not very big, and it's in the middle of everything noisy.")
❑ Commuter's dream ("The off-ramp leads right to your front door.")
❑ Convenient to shopping ("During Christmas, your front yard becomes a parking lot.")
❑ Country living (See "Off the beaten path," below.)
❑ Cozy and affordable (See "Great starter home," below.)
❑ Distress sale ("We're distressed because we can't sell it.")
❑ Great starter home ("Tiny, and priced accordingly.")
❑ Handyman's special ("Bring a hammer, perhaps even a bull-dozer.")
❑ Hurry! ("We're tired of trying to sell this one.")
❑ Immaculate condition ("We've washed the windows and waxed the kitchen floor.)
❑ Must see to appreciate ("Looks better outside than inside.")
❑ Off the beaten path ("Far from everything.")
❑ Owner must sell ("Of course. Otherwise it wouldn't be listed here.")
❑ Picture book setting ("You can see trees from the kitchen window.")
❑ Walk to downtown ("You'll learn to ignore the traffic noise.")
❑ Won't last the weekend ("Our listing on it expires soon.")

You get the idea. The long and short of it is that you should probably just ignore such breathless claims. Listing agents rely on these and many other stock phrases to make their properties stand out in the crowd, but they usually have little to do with the specifics of the actual property.

HOW TO INSPECT A HOUSE
When it comes time for you to look at houses, you will first go on your own or with an agent to look at prospective properties, or

just to get a feel for the market. You'll rule out some properties right away, perhaps even before you get out of your car. But some will be of interest— at least for a while. And you'll want to learn how to look these properties over thoroughly but relatively quickly. As you get serious about a particular property, you can inspect it in greater detail, and bring in an independent home inspector to do a professional job.

You will be looking at four key aspects of the property:

❑ Whether it offers the space, layout, and features you need.
❑ The desirability of the neighborhood and location.
❑ The important faults or defects that may create problems for you now or later on.
❑ How much it will cost you to own and maintain.

We're not concerned quite yet with the structure and mechanical systems of the house. For now, you're only giving the property a once over for livability. Here are some of the first things you'll want to consider:

❑ Is the floor plan well laid out with separate areas for working, living, and sleeping?
❑ Are the rooms large enough to accommodate your possessions? You don't need a tape measure to judge room sizes. Simply pace the length and width of the room; an average pace is about a yard. (If you want to be more precise, take ten normal paces at home and measure the distance you covered, then divide by ten to determine the distance of one typical pace.)
❑ Is the traffic pattern appropriate for your family? Where and how will children enter? Will the dining room get used as a hallway? Are there bathrooms where needed?
❑ Are the kitchen appliances relatively up to date? Are there the ones you need, including a dishwasher and disposal? Is it laid out well for you, with workable cooking and cleanup areas? Is there adequate counter, cabinet, and storage space?
❑ Are eating areas convenient to the kitchen?
❑ Is there adequate storage?
❑ Is there an adequate yard to accommodate your lifestyle, children, and pets?

❑ Are there enough bathrooms—both full bathrooms (those with bath or shower) and half bathrooms (those without)?
❑ Is there a garage, if necessary?
❑ Does the house feel "right"?

This last question, admittedly, is somewhat ambiguous— after all, what does the "right" house feel like?—but it is worth asking yourself nonetheless. If you have a good or bad feeling right from the start, that can go a long way toward an early decision. If it doesn't feel good, even if it seems in decent shape and the price is reasonable, it's best to move on to the next property. If it does feel good, even if it's going to need some work, or you might have to stretch your budget a bit to make the numbers work, it's probably worth pursuing, assuming that you do it in a responsible manner.

INSPECTING FROM THE GROUND UP

If you do like the location, style, layout, and feel of a particular property, your next move is to take a good thorough look at it. You'll still want to bring along a professional inspector later on, but this next inspection will be key to deciding whether to make an offer and, if so, for how much. In making the inspection, you might want to bring along a friend or some other person. Two heads usually are better than one. In any case, you should make sure to have a flashlight, pen and paper, and a tape measure. You probably should wear something you don't mind getting dirty.

In making your inspection, the key rule is to

❑ open
❑ close
❑ look into
❑ look behind
❑ operate

everything. You want to look for hidden flaws, cracks, blemishes, and defects, as well as the less-hidden things. Don't be shy. If the house is on the market for sale, it is there to be inspected thoroughly, assuming that you don't cause any damage to the property itself, or otherwise endanger yourself or others.

As you find things, whether or not you're certain if they are a problem, jot them down in your notebook, no matter how trivial they may seem. It all adds up. You want to get a reasonably good fix on how much money it will cost you to remedy any and all problems.

Let's start at the bottom and work our way up.

Outside the House

Among the areas to examine carefully:

❑ *Foundation, grading, and drainage.* You want to check for holes, cracks, or unevenness. Are there any cracks or porous areas in the foundation walls? Is the floor even? Water is a house's worst enemy. If there is not proper drainage, water will build up in and around the house, causing severe damage to its structure. Settlement causes some water problems: Some homes have what builders call "negative pitch," a common phenomenon even among newer homes, where fluffed-up soil subsides over time and surface water runs back toward the house. Look at the ground to make sure it slopes away from the house. If water doesn't lead away from the house, it will make its way inside.

❑ *Driveway and sidewalks.* Again, you're looking for holes and cracks. Are the surfaces—the driveway, walkway, patios, and sidewalks—in good condition, or must they be resurfaced?

❑ *Grounds.* Aside from its size, is the land in good shape? If it appears eroded or contains sunken portions, it may indicate a drainage problem. Is there enough topsoil for planting new grass (about five inches), shrubs (at least eighteen inches), and trees (at least two feet)? If the front or backyard is not well taken care of, it may provide an indication of the present and previous owners' general wear and tear on the house. If there are fences, look for holes, loose or missing sections, or rotted posts.

❑ *Critters and pests.* These can range from rats and termites to a long list of tiny little things that can take up residence in a house or environs, any of which could make your life as a homeowner less than rosy. Termites are one of the biggest pests, but you probably won't see any obvious signs of infestation unless you're a trained professional. Later on, before you settle on the property, you'll have a professional termite inspection done; most (but not all) lenders require it. That inspection should also cover carpenter ants and other wood-boring pests. In general, houses don't have termites if there is not water problem, the foundation is poured concrete, exposed wood is at least one foot off the ground, and there is no old wood sitting around rotting.

❑ *Outside steps.* These can be another sign of a bad foundation, improper drainage, or otherwise shaky ground. When a house settles or shifts, the outside steps often don't move with it, leaving gaps between steps, or between the steps and the house. And once they do separate, there is great potential for problems as water gets into the cracks, freezes and thaws.

❑ *Brick work.* Look for cracks and loose or missing mortar. If there's a chimney, look for loose or missing bricks. Obviously, the chimney, when seen from outside, shouldn't be tilting.

❑ *Outside appearance.* If the house has siding— clapboards, shingles, or other materials— look for loose or missing pieces, lifting, or warping. If it's painted, look for peeling, chipping, or blistering.

❑ *Gutters and downspouts.* Check for missing sections, gaps, or holes in the joints. Gutters and downspouts should remove all water at least two feet from the house itself. Look for signs that water may be running down the side of the house, indicating that gutters or spouts are blocked or broken.

❑ *Outside lighting.* Is there adequate lighting in the front and back to provide both illumination and security?

❑ *Garage.* Check the doors, roof, siding, and windows.

❑ *Roof.* A roof needs to be repaired or replaced several times during the lifetime of a house, so it's important to know the kind of roofing used and its condition. The life expectancy of roofing depends on the material:

asphalt rolls	10 years
built-up roofing	10-20 years
wood shingles	10-40 years
asphalt shingles	15-20 years
asphalt interlocking shingles	15-25 years
metal roofing	15-40 years
clay tiles	20+ years
asphalt multi-thickness shingles	20-30 years
asbestos cement shingles	30-75 years
slate shingles	30-100 years

You should inquire whether the existing roof includes a warranty that may be transferred to a new owner.

Inside the House

So much for the outside. Now, let's go inside and take a look around. Again, we'll start at the bottom and work our way up.

BASEMENT
Any part of the house that's below ground is subject to leaking, and a leaky house is not something to fool around with; it's one of the most serious problems of home ownership. In a perfect world, you would conduct your inspection right after a rainstorm, enabling you to inspect for leaks and seepage, but that's usually not possible. (Besides, even the brightest of houses looks dreary on a rainy day, and you'll get an unfair impression.)

What are the signs of a leaky basement? You'll have to use your senses: it will smell, look, or feel damp. You'll probably notice the musty smell as soon as you enter the basement. You'll see stains, streaks, or spots on the walls and floor. You might find loose tiles or warped flooring. And if the condition is bad enough, it will simply *feel* damp.

Don't just take a cursory look around. It's important to look under and behind things, and to move large objects that might be hiding evidence of leakiness. Be suspicious if the basement is freshly painted: It might be a sign of a well-manicured residence, but it could also indicate that someone's trying to hide something. And beware if the basement has the just-cleaned odor of Pinesol or some other cleaning substance; it may have been scrubbed down just before you arrived.

UTILITIES

If the house has a basement, this is where you'll probably find a number of key mechanical components, including the water heater, the heating and air conditioning systems, the water supply, and the electrical system. If not in the basement, they will be elsewhere, perhaps attached to the outside of the house on the side or in back. Let's look at each:

❑ The *water heater* should be large enough for your family's use. For a family of three, that means at least fifty gallons; if larger, at least sixty-five gallons. It should be well insulated, as should the pipes going out of it carrying hot water throughout the house. A timer, enabling it to cycle on during the day and off at night, is recommended. Inspect the water heater carefully. It shouldn't show any signs of leaks or rust. Check, too, on the water heater's age; they typically have a life span of about fifteen to twenty years. If it's on the last third of that life span, keep in mind that it will need replacing sooner rather than later.

❑ The *plumbing* isn't easy to check if you're not an expert, but you can at least ask some questions, particularly if the house is more than thirty years old. Many homes built during the housing boom that followed World War II contain brass or copper pipes, the life span of which is about forty years. In other words, their replacement time may be imminent. And an overhaul of the plumbing system can be one of the costliest fix-up jobs you'll do in a house.

Beyond that, you should do a superficial inspection for leaks and rust. Try all the toilets and sinks, particularly those on the top floor if it's a multilevel house. You might try running several sinks, or flushing several toilets, at once, to see how much that affects the water pressure. It should have some effect, but it shouldn't reduce water flow to a trickle. If the water pressure isn't good, there's a decent chance there's a big plumbing job on the horizon. Look also for clogged or sluggish drains and dripping faucets.

As for the adequacy of the water supply— the quantity and quality of water flowing into the house— that will be difficult to check on your own. You'll likely need a professional housing inspector to help make those determinations.

❑ The *heating system* can be a money burner if it's not efficient or adequate. Find out what type of heat— forced air, hot water, or steam— the system uses, and what the energy source is— oil, natural gas, or electricity. In most parts of the country, natural gas is the least expensive energy source, followed by oil and then electricity. But don't count out an all-electric home: While they can be relatively expensive to heat and cool, many all-electric homes are better insulated and contain more energy-saving features, such as heat pumps. Another consideration when it comes to energy sources is planning for the future: electricity-based systems typically run on oil- and nuclear-powered electric utilities; oil-based systems may be subject to the vagaries of international politics.

As with the water heater, the age of the "heating plant," as the central heating unit is known, is important to know. System life tends to range between 15 and 18 years; a heat pump's life is usually a few years shorter than that of a gas- or oil-fired furnace. In general, newer models are much more energy efficient than older ones. If it's a newer model, ask for the energy efficiency rating, or EER, a measurement of appliance energy costs that comes with new heating and air conditioning units, among other appliances.

The best measurement of heating system efficiency, of course, is to see a year's worth of utility bills— electricity, oil, and gas, as appropriate. But that may not be possible if you're looking at an already vacated house.

❑ The *electrical system* is another behind-the-walls network that can be costly to overhaul. In general, the older the house, the more likely it is to carry inadequate electrical service. What you want to know is amperage. If you're a typical household, with a few kitchen appliances, a washer and dryer, and an assortment of TVs, stereos, VCRs, clocks, reading lamps, electric tooth-brushes, and hair dryers, you'll require at least 100-amp service. If the house has central air conditioning, make that 200 amps. Many houses built before the mid-1950s, unless they have been upgraded, carry only 60 amps of service. This probably will not be adequate if you live a modern lifestyle.

Are there enough electrical outlets in each room? In many older homes, there may be only one or two outlets, which may be insufficient for your needs. (You might want to take a look at a few rooms in your present house to see how many things you've got plugged in. You'll probably be surprised at how many things there are.) Keep in mind that adding even a single outlet or wiring for an overhead light fixture or fan can run upwards of $1,000.

Another major concern is aluminum wiring, which was commonly used in houses built between 1965 and 1973. In recent years, aluminum wiring has been found to be a major fire hazard, causing the federal government to declare it an "imminent hazard" in more than a million and a half homes. (Aluminum wiring installed after 1973 isn't considered to be a problem.) The fire hazard stems from the way aluminum wiring of that period was connected to outlets and switches, causing them to overheat. Owners of such wiring have been strongly advised to have it repaired or replaced— again, a costly endeavor. If the house you're considering was built during that period, it would be a good idea to have an independent housing inspector or electri-cian examine it.

❏ The *air conditioning* system, if there is one, should be large enough to cool the entire house. It should work quietly and efficiently and, ideally, should have a high EER. This will be difficult to check unless you are able to visit the house during the dog days of summer. Again, an examination of actual utility bills is your best bet.

FLOORS, WALLS, WINDOWS, AND DOORS
You needn't be a carpenter to appreciate good craftsmanship.

You need only use your eyes. When looking at these structural elements of a house, one of your main criteria will be: Does it appear well built?

❏ *Floors* should feel solid. Jump up and down on them a couple of times. Does the floor give a little or remain firm? Most floors, particularly in older homes, seem to creak a little, so don't let this put you off unless it is excessive and widespread. Look for the levelness of floors, as well as bowing, movement, and looseness when you walk around. Also check their surface condition. Are wooden floorboards cracked, stained, or loose? Are linoleum tiles discolored or missing? Are bathroom tiles in good shape?

❏ *Walls* should feel sound and smooth. If they are plaster walls and ceilings, check for cracking. If they're excessively cracked or peeling, they will like need to be scraped, patched, and painted before they are presentable. If there's excessive cracking, it may indicate water leakage. Check wallpapered and painted walls: Will their colors and patterns suit you, or will you need to replace/repaint them soon? Those costs should be factored into your cost estimates.

❏ *Doors* should open and close with ease. While there may be some seasonal stickiness due to summer humidity or winter dryness, doors shouldn't require strenuous pulling. Check also the condition of door screens or glass panels that may not be installed due to the time of year. Don't forget locks: Are they adequate for your safety and comfort? Do all outside locks require the same key, or are several keys needed to open the front, back, side, and garage doors? What about storm doors? In colder regions, these can go a long way toward saving energy.

❏ *Windows* are one of the biggest energy wasters in a house if they're inadequate or poorly fitting. Indeed, about two-thirds of all heat loss in houses is through windows and doors. Most older houses have single-paned windows, which may be inadequate for today's energy costs; the price of installing double-paned (two thicknesses of glass with a small air space in between) or storm (a second window installed outside the first) windows is costly, but it may pay off over time in reduced fuel bills and, of course, will provide greater comfort in keeping heat in during winter and out during summer.

The cost of replacing broken or badly working windows can be high, so it's important to check these thoroughly. Are the windows cracked, scratched, or broken? Are the window screens in good condition (if it's winter, they might not be installed)? You can't adequately check windows without testing them. Even if they appear in good condition, the sashes or frames may be warped or broken, leaking in cold air (or, in summer, hot air) and water. Do they open and close with ease? Do their locking mechanisms work well? Are they decent locks for your comfort and security?

What about shades and drapes? Are existing ones adequate or will you need to purchase them? Again, these can have energy-saving implications as well as aesthetic ones: the right window treatments can keep harsh sun out during summer months and can help keep heat inside during winter months.

Consider also the passive solar aspects of the house— for example, how the sun shines in the windows (or doesn't) and how that might affect comfort and warmth. If the house and its windows are oriented so that the sun comes glaring into the house during summer afternoons— or doesn't come through at all during cold winter days—that's good to know. (You can partly remedy the sun's unwanted rays in summer using shades and other devices; to bring the sun in would require building a skylight or adding windows.)

Solar energy considerations aside, how much direct sunlight do you get? How important is this to you? Remember that, as mentioned above, the position of the sun in relation to the house will change throughout the year.

THE REST OF THE HOUSE

❏ *Insulation.* While we're on the subject of energy, you should be aware of the amount and type of insulation in the house's ceilings and walls. This will probably not be an easy task— after all, the insulation is behind the walls and ceiling. But the owner or real estate agent should be able to give you some indication of insulation, ideally expressed as an "R" factor, a standardized term that describes a wall or ceiling's resistance to hot and cold air passing through. For example, in the cold Midwest, a house should ideally have R-19 insulation, the equivalent of about four inches of fiberglass insulation in the ceiling.

Because heat rises, the most important insulation is in the attic or, if there's no attic, between the top floor and the roof. In most parts of the country, you'll need about a foot of insulation, offering an energy efficiency rating of between R-22 and R-30. There are a host of other energy-saving measures, from sealing up door jambs and covering hot-water pipes to the use of aforementioned storm windows and storm doors. The idea is that the "tighter" a house is sealed against escaping air, the less energy it will waste.

But not *too* tight. It's important that a house be able to breathe, lest it build up humidity, odors, pollutants and, in the summer, heat. In the rush to save energy, overly tight houses can result in anything from structural damage to poor health conditions for its occupants.

The type of insulation is important, too. Be particularly on the lookout for asbestos. Many homes constructed between 1958 and 1970 used asbestos fibers, mostly for fireproofing and thermal insulation. Over the years, the asbestos fibers have begun to come loose. Asbestos is a cancer-causing substance, and the Environmental Protection Agency has determined that there is no safe level. Removing asbestos insulation and replacing it with something less harmful is a very costly measure.

At this point, it is important only to be aware in these broad ways of the energy-saving (or energy-wasting) features of a prospective house. You will get additional information from the professional inspector you hire before you make your purchase.

❑ *Kitchen.* You may not be surprised to learn that the kitchen is the room most scrutinized by the majority of buyers. And with good reason: There is much here that affects livability, and so much that must jibe with individuals' habits and lifestyles.

Having an up-to-date kitchen is an important feature— not just to you, but to your ability to get a good price for the house when you sell it some day. Ideally, a kitchen will have:

✔ adequate counter space
✔ adequate cabinet space
✔ good layout
✔ good ventilation (including a window over the sink)
✔ modern appliances (including dishwasher and garbage dis-
      posal)
    ✔ adequate electrical outlets
    ✔ a sizable pantry
    ✔ modern flooring
    ✔ a bright and sunny feel

Kitchens can be improved or rebuilt, of course, but it's not inexpensive. Even a basic spruce-up can cost $10,000.

❑ *Bathrooms.* These are the next most important rooms in the house, at least as far as attractiveness to buyers is concerned. Tiny, plain bathrooms— the kind found in most older houses— stand out like a sore thumb. And making major improvements to bathrooms can be even more expensive than renovating kitchens, given the costly plumbing chores involved. So, unless you're planning to sink bucks into your newly purchased house, plan to be stuck with the bathrooms as they are, at least for the first few years. First, look at the number and placement around the house: Are there enough for your family, and are they located near enough to bedrooms, living room, and kitchen, or other appropriate locations? Is there adequate privacy, from both the inside and out? Are the bathroom appliances shiny and modern, or are there stains and cracks in the sink and tub? Are the wall and floor tiles intact, or are they loose, chipped, cracked, or missing? Is there adequate counter and cabinet space? Proper ventilation? As with kitchens, this will be a highly subjective determination.

❑ *Bedrooms.* Simply put, the more the better. Whether or not you are married with children, ideally you want enough rooms for the occupants and their visiting family and friends. Those guest rooms, of course, will be taken over for a wide range of activities, between visits by guests: TV watching, sewing, hobbies, busi-ness, exercise, or the ever-popular storage (read: junk). But despite your quest for a maximum of such rooms, be wary of bedroom claims by real estate agents and ads: What they call a potential "bedroom" is often a glorified closet. So, that four-bedroom house you are looking at might have only three—or even two—rooms that you consider adequate for use as a bedroom by your family. Check also for closet space: To be a fully qualified bedroom, it should have enough space for clothes storage that its occupant needn't go down the hall to get dressed.

The location of bedrooms is important, too. Ideally, they should be far enough away from the general family living space to provide adequate privacy.

❑ *Living room.* Its adequacy will have a lot to do with how much you entertain and whether there is another room—a family room, rec room, or den, for example—in which you and your family will do the bulk of your TV-watching, reading, and conversing. Ideally, it should be laid out so that when you walk through the front door, there is an entranceway or some other space before you reach the living room.

❑ *Fireplace.* If the house has a fireplace, you should check it carefully. Does the damper work? Has the chimney been cleaned out recently? (It probably hasn't; very few sellers consider doing this to enhance a home's resale value.)

❑ *Storage.* Having a lot of storage space is either a necessity or a luxury, depending on your particular lifestyle. If there isn't enough storage space presently, at least make sure that there are other spaces, like a dry basement or attic, that can be converted into storage space at a reasonable cost. These needn't be behemoth spaces adequate to fit your entire collection of old college textbooks. You may require only one additional closet for linens and winter clothes, carved out of one of the existing bedrooms. The important thing is to determine how much you'll need (probably at least 50 percent more than you have presently) and make sure it's available for your use in your new house.

❑ *Other rooms.* The need for these will vary widely, including the previously mentioned family room, recreation room, dining

room, den, deck, porch (fully enclosed, screened-in, or open),
laundry room, workshop, office, and on and on. In each case,
you'll have to decide whether the number, size, and layout of
these rooms meets the needs and desires you noted in Chapter
2.

❏ *Other amenities.* Make sure you understand what else comes
with the house and what doesn't. Does that full-length mirror in
the bedroom remain? How about the living room drapes? Do all
the appliances convey to the new owner, or does that auxiliary
freezer in the garage go with the present owners? A full inventory of items should be included in the purchase contract, but for
now, you should be aware of exactly what you might be buying.

PROPERTY TAXES

One expense often overlooked by potential homeowners is property taxes. In most cities and towns, property taxes add an ever-
growing amount to home ownership, as municipalities dig increasingly deeper for funds for police, firefighters, street cleaners, street lights, and all the rest.

So, knowing how much tax you'll have to pay each year for
a particular piece of property is key to annual housing costs.
Taxes vary widely— from over $1,000 in some of the highest-
taxed areas to under $100 in a few places. The exact amount is
usually determined by taxing the assessed value of a home—
that is, the value placed on the home for tax purposes by the local
city or county assessor. Then, a tax rate is applied to that value.
So, for example, if the tax rate is $1 per $100 of assessed value,
that would mean an annual tax of $1,000 for a house assessed at
$100,000. (Note that assessed value and actual value may be far
different. In some areas, the assessed value is only a third of the
actual market value.) Taxes may be due quarterly, semiannu-
ally, or annually, depending on the local jurisdiction. The good
news, however, is that property taxes are deductible in your
federal tax returns, and in many state tax returns, too.

There are two ways to get an accurate determination of the
amount of property tax you'll have to pay on a given house. The
easiest way is to look at the most recent tax receipts or bills from
the previous owners. That won't necessarily be the amount you'll

pay, as tax rates and appraised values rise, often annually. But it will give you a pretty close figure. Another way is to call or visit the local assessor's office to determine the current tax rate and the appraised value of the property in question. Both figures are part of the public record. If you're moving to a new city, you should be aware that some cities also have local income taxes. This will be in addition to state and federal taxes.

A Second Look

If you've done your job thoroughly, you've taken in quite a bit of information during your inspection— much more information, in fact, than you can keep track of easily, particularly after you've inspected more than one house. It will help to keep some written records, perhaps rating each component of each house on a 1-to-10 or A-to-F scale.

But don't rely on only one visit to make your determination. Go back a second, third, or fourth time if necessary. You are making a *major* purchase— the biggest one you'll probably ever make (not including your *next* house)— and there's no reason not to have all the information you'll need to make an informed decision. And keep in mind that before you make the final purchase, you'll have the house gone over carefully by a professional inspector.

Before we get on with the process of wheeling and dealing on a house that passes muster, let's get down to the nitty-gritty matter of dollars and cents.

Chapter 4
Money Talks

It isn't necessary to have money in your pocket to go house-hunting— indeed, you can't even get a mortgage until you have a contract on a specific property— but you should have some idea of how you're going to get it. So, before we go further into the house-buying process, it's time to look at the realities of real estate financing.

The sad state of the world is such that, our American way of justice notwithstanding, when you seek a mortgage, you're considered "guilty until proven innocent." That is, until you are able to prove beyond a reasonable doubt that you will be able to make the monthly payments on your mortgage, it's assumed that you're something of a deadbeat. Forget the fact that mortgage lending is a pretty competitive field, and that there is a lot of money to be made by lenders who succeed in getting your business. Their approach generally remains the same: "We don't believe you can do it until you show us otherwise."

This is not altogether unreasonable. After all, from their point of view, we're talking about lending a princely sum to a veritable stranger. So the lender needs to know about you: your financial situation—past, present, and future—your credit history, and a few things about the house you're buying, among other things.

Still, the process is unnecessarily long. It can take weeks and weeks to get a mortgage commitment, a time period that seems excessive in these days of computers and lightning-fast communications technology. Credit checks can be done in a matter of minutes; employment and income verification can be done with a phone call for most people. And a reasonably accurate value of the property can be determined with minimum effort.

So what takes so long? Part of it has to do with habit. "That's the way we've always done it," is how one lender explained it.

Part of it has to do with backlog: During times of low or rising interest rates, lenders often are flooded with mortgage applicants trying to take advantage of the situation. So there are bottlenecks. Sometimes, the delay has to do with getting all of the information— the appraisal, some financial documents from you or your mortgage co-signer, if you have one. And a lot of it has to do with the fact that the wheels of justice grind slowly.

Fortunately, there are signs that this apparent foot-dragging lending style is changing. In 1989, Citicorp, one of the nation's largest mortgage lenders, began offering something revolutionary: mortgage commitments in *fifteen minutes*. That's right, a quarter of an hour, or less than the time it takes to fill out the application. The quick commitments, legally binding on the bank and requiring only correct information and a satisfactory appraisal, are part of what may well be a new era of competitiveness, or it could be a short-lived marketing stunt. Whatever the motive behind them, Citicorp's fast and firm commitments point up the reality of mortgage lending: It needn't take forever and a day to qualify for a mortgage.

The best thing to keep in mind is that there are millions of mortgages made every year. In fact, of the 4 million or so home sales made every year in the United States, only 3 percent are paid for fully in cash; the rest have mortgages. So take heart.

It would be possible to create a book on this subject alone; indeed, there are several books that deal solely with how to get a mortgage. And with good reason: House financing is a complex area, becoming increasingly so, thanks to a never-ending list of new financial instruments, lending institutions, and tax laws. In this chapter, we'll go through the basic process and examine a few of the many types of mortgages available. When it comes time for you to apply for a mortgage, you are urged to consult your financial advisers to get the most up-to-date information.

HOW MUCH SHOULD YOU BORROW?

One of the most common dilemmas faced by home buyers— particularly first-time buyers— is how much to borrow and how much to use as a down payment. Do you put down as little as you possibly can, thereby having a larger mortgage with bigger monthly payments— but also more cash in your bank account—

or do you make a larger down payment and have smaller monthly payments, enabling you to keep more of each paycheck?

The answer has a little to do with your financial philosophy and a lot to do with your financial situation. To figure out what's best, it will help to go through some of the same type of calculations that a lender goes through to determine your ability to carry a mortgage of a given size. One of the first things the lender will want to know is your net worth: the amount of money you would have if you were to sell everything you own and pay off all your debts today. A sample net worth statement is shown below. Be realistic when filling it out. It won't help you to exaggerate your assets or "forget" about a few outstanding debts. You'll do best by disclosing all.

NET WORTH STATEMENT

Assets		Liabilities		
			Unpaid Balance	**Monthly Payment**
Liquid Assets				
Cash (checking)	$_____	Real estate	$_____	$_____
Cash (savings)	$_____		$_____	$_____
Stocks/bonds[1]	$_____	Automobiles	$_____	$_____
Life insurance[2]	$_____		$_____	$_____
		Charge	$_____	$_____
Illiquid Assets		accounts	$_____	$_____
Real Estate[1]	$_____		$_____	$_____
	$_____		$_____	$_____
Automobiles[1]	$_____		$_____	$_____
	$_____	Alimony	$_____	$_____
Household goods	$_____	Child support	$_____	$_____
Other	$_____	Other	$_____	$_____
	$_____		$_____	$_____
	$_____		$_____	$_____
Total	$_____	**Total**	$_____	$_____

[1] Market value.
[2] Cash value.

As you can see, there are two kinds of assets: liquid assets— those you can easily convert to cash, including money in checking and savings accounts, stocks and bonds, and certain other investments, and illiquid assets— those that would take some time to convert to cash, including cars, furniture, real estate, a stamp collection, and investments such as limited partnerships, for which there is no ready market.

It's those liquid assets that we'll be considering for purposes of buying a house; the illiquid ones simply aren't worth considering as available during the time-sensitive period between making an offer on a house and going to settlement. (If you find it necessary to raise more cash before you can buy, it may be necessary to liquidate some of your illiquid assets; then, you can add that to the liquid assets on your net worth statement.)

Now, let's do some calculations using those figures for your liquid assets:

FINDING THE DOWN PAYMENT MONEY*

Money you have on hand:

Savings accounts	$_____
Equity in your home	$_____
Anticipated savings	$_____
Other liquid assets	$_____

1.   **Total money on hand** $_____

Money you can borrow:

Insurance policies	$_____
Loans from family	$_____
Personal note	$_____
Credit card loans	$_____
Credit union loan	$_____
Other loans	$_____
	$_____

2.   **Total borrowing ability** $_____

Total Money Available   (1 + 2) $_____

*It may help to consult the net worth statement you calculated earlier in this chapter to obtain some of the figures for this calculation.

The bottom line is the amount of money you already have available for a down payment. If that number seems depressingly low, don't despair: there are several additional things you can do to increase your down payment, which we'll get to in a moment. But first, let's look at the advantages and disadvantages of large and small down payments.

❑*Advantages of a small down payment.* Look at a down payment as a kind of lever— it is a relatively small sum of money that enables you to buy a much more expensive item, the house. If you pay only a small portion of the house's cost in cash, it's like using a lever with a long handle to lift something— you get a lot of leverage. So, if you're making a 5 percent down payment on a $100,000 house, you're using $5,000 to get you something that costs twenty times more. Clearly, then, one advantage of a small down payment is that a little money can go a long way.

To fully appreciate the value of leveraging, let's look at what happens when the value of your house appreciates. If that $100,000 house goes up in value at 5 percent a year over three years— to a total of $115,762— you've tripled your money: You put down $5,000 and made a $15,000 profit, at least when you sell the house. On an annualized basis, your investment made 105 percent a year for three years. (We'll leave closing costs out of the equation for the sake of simplicity). If you had made a $10,000 down payment, you would have realized a 150 percent profit, or a 52.5 percent annual return; if you had made a $20,000 down payment, your "profit" would be 75 percent, or 26.25 percent on an annual basis. (That's still not bad, considering that a savings account pays a measly 5 percent or so.)

Leveraging, then, makes good sense. Where else can you make a 105 percent profit a year on a $5,000 investment? Another way to put it is that you can get more house for less money. While that sounds illogical, consider that if you have $10,000 to spend, you can get a $50,000 house (at a 20 percent down payment), a $100,000 house (at a 10 percent down payment) or a $200,000 house (at a 5 percent down payment). Given the choice, which would you want?

There are a lot of real estate experts who strongly suggest to put down the least amount of money you can get away with and to get the biggest mortgage you can possibly afford. Uncle Sam agrees. Under tax laws, the federal government essentially encourages larger mortgages. By maintaining your ability to deduct fully any interest paid on the mortgage for your principal residence, but limiting the amount of money you can deduct on a home-equity loan, the government was saying, "Better to borrow the most you can now, because if you want to borrow more later on, you might not be able to deduct all the interest on your taxes."

Another advantage of making a small down payment is that you'll have more cash on hand to pay for other things, including fixing up your new house, which will likely further increase its value. If you wanted to get a home-improvement loan to do that same work, you'd later have to pay an interest rate several percentage points higher than your mortgage. Mortgages, simply put, are the least expensive forms of money you can borrow.

❏ *Disadvantages of a small down payment.* Life isn't all roses for those who make smaller down payments. For one thing, lenders are more reluctant to give mortgages to those who make small down payments, so you'll have to make a good case when it comes to demonstrating to a lender that you can easily afford the monthly payments. From a lender's point of view, there is less incentive for you to pay your mortgage every month if you own say, only 5 percent of the house, because it won't be as much of a loss if you are forced to walk away from the house and leave the lender with the burden of foreclosing on the property, selling the house, and getting repaid from the proceeds. The more you put down, the bigger your stake, and the better the lender feels about your commitment to making timely payments.

To make them feel better about a small down payment, lenders generally require those who put down less than 20 percent to pay for private mortgage insurance, or PMI. That policy, the cost of which is added on to your monthly payments, protects the lender if you default on the loan. PMI will add about one quarter of one percent to your interest rate, along with a lump-sum payment of one percent of the amount you borrow at the time of settlement.

❏ *Advantages of a larger down payment.* Obviously, the more money you put down, the less you'll have to borrow, and therefore the lower your monthly payment. That's one advantage of a larger down payment. Another is that a loan of 80 percent or less of the purchase price of the house is easier to get than a loan greater than 80 percent—lenders will more readily commit their money when you commit a healthy portion of yours. The larger down payment will also save you money on points—one point equals one percent of the amount you borrow; borrowers typically pay two or three points on a loan, which can add up to quite a sum—because you'll be borrowing a smaller amount. And you won't have to pay private mortgage insurance.

Putting more money down certainly makes sense if you have some cash and an unstable monthly income. By keeping your monthly payment to a minimum, you'll lower the risk of running into problems meeting payments. And if you're nervous about borrowing money in the first place, which a lot of people are, having lower monthly payments might provide some peace of mind.

Remember that the advice of the experts mentioned above was to put down the least amount of money you can get away with and to get the biggest mortgage you can possibly afford. The key word here is *afford.* If you can only afford to pay a monthly mortgage equal to about 75 percent of the price of the house you're buying, then you should find some way to make a 25 percent down payment.

❏ *Disadvantages of a larger down payment.* The disadvantages should be obvious by now: You have to come up with a big chunk of cash, possibly tens of thousands of dollars, not to mention thousands more in closing costs. This simply isn't possible for most first-time buyers. Even if you have the money, it might make more sense to save your cash for other things, including home repairs, emergencies, and other investments.

VA AND FHA MORTGAGES

Uncle Sam has always encouraged home ownership, and two of his programs can be very helpful to first-time buyers, both of which you apply for through a lending institution.

❑ **VA loans** are available to qualified veterans of the armed services and are partly guaranteed by the Veterans Administration. What makes VA loans so attractive is that they require *nothing* down. Moreover, they are relatively easy to apply for and get, unlike some other government programs for home buyers. The maximum amount of these loans is set on a case-by-case basis by VA-authorized appraisers. Also quite attractive is that VA loans, which are typically at low interest rates, can be transferred to a subsequent buyer, assuming he or she is credit worthy, whether the buyer is a veteran or not. That raises the value of your home for resale purposes.

❑ **FHA loans** are insured by the Federal Housing Administration, a part of the Department of Housing and Urban Development. FHA was the first insurer of mortgages—since these insured loans were created by Congress in 1934, a number of *private* mortgage insurers have since opened their doors—and once insured one of every four mortgages; the number is now about half that. FHA loans are insured up to $90,000 (the actual amount depends on an area's housing prices) and require down payments of as little as 3 percent. The bad news about FHA loans is that they require a tremendous amount of red tape and can slow up the approval process by several weeks. Moreover, FHA points above 1 point must be paid by the seller. As a result of all these oddities is that many lenders and sellers simply avoid dealing with FHA loans.

One problem with both VA and FHA loans is that because their interest rates are usually below market, lenders will usually make up some of the difference by charging you points— often as many as three or four. That requires some up-front cash, which slightly offsets the low- or no-down payment advantages these loans offer. Both loans also have limits as to how much can be insured or guaranteed, which may place a ceiling on the price of the house you can afford.

Coming Up with the Cash

VA and FHA loans are designed specifically to overcome a major obstacle for first-time buyers: problem coming up with the sizable chunk of cash needed to make the down payment and closing costs. Not many people have $20,000 or more sitting around waiting to be tapped. Indeed, the lack of cash is a stumbling block for a lot of would-be home buyers with otherwise sufficient income.

Other than VA and FHA loans, how can you find money you don't already have? There are several options:

❑ *Second mortgages.* "Seconds," as they are called, are exactly that: an additional mortgage on top of your principal one. The second mortgage is usually for a much smaller amount and for a much shorter time period— $10,000 or $20,000 for five to ten years, for example. They will also likely be at a higher interest rate. Unless you have substantial regular income, you aren't likely to get a second mortgage from a traditional mortgage lender; a better bet would be through your real estate agent or the seller.

❑ *Alternative mortgages.* There are almost as many alternative mortgage arrangements as there are houses for sale. Some of them feature low down payments, with monthly payments rising in later years to compensate. More about those in a moment.

❑ *Seller financing.* It's increasingly common that the seller participate in the financing. Of course, there must be something in it for the seller; sometimes that "something" is simply making it easier to sell the property. There are a variety of ways the seller may help—by deferring part of the down payment for a few years, for example; or by lending you the money for the down payment as a "balloon" loan, in which case you would pay only the interest portion for, say, five years, at which time the principal comes due in a lump sum. Of course, you're betting on the assumption that you'll be in better financial shape in five years and will have that chunk of cash then. But then again, you can worry about that later. (Of course, if you aren't in better financial shape when the balloon comes due, you'll have to devise another plan, perhaps find another balloon loan. The risk is that interest rates or your own financial situation might make it impossible for you to qualify for any suitable loan, with the risk that you'll have to sell your home to pay off the balloon.) Another advantage of your having the seller financing part of the down payment is that it may qualify you for an 80 percent mortgage, meaning you'll save having to pay for private mortgage insurance.

MORTGAGES MADE SIMPLER

As stated at the beginning of this chapter, the mortgage-lending community generally doesn't make borrowing an enjoyable experience. And the mere thought of borrowing $50,000 or $100,000 may leave a knot in your stomach. But the more you know, the less distressing the process will be.

One thing to keep in mind is that while the traditional thirty-year fixed-rate mortgage—in which your monthly payment remains the same until the loan is paid off or you sell the house— is still the most common, there are many other types of mortgages. The idea is to find one that will best fit your financial situation and sense of financial security. Another thing to remember is that lenders are in the business to lend. Despite how they may treat you, they *want* to give you a mortgage. And for lenders, there is no safer risk than to give a mortgage; it's far less risky than a car loan or even a checking overdraft credit limit, although the amount is certainly greater.

The amount you will pay each month for your mortgage includes four items:

❑ **Principal**— a portion of the amount you borrowed
❑ **Interest**— the "price" of the loan
❑ **Taxes**— a portion of your property taxes, paid each month into escrow
❑ **Insurance**— also paid into an escrow account

These four items are usually known by the acronym PITI. In most mortgages, the first two items—principal and interest—remain the same for the life of the mortgage, while the other two items—taxes and insurance—usually go up.

Mortgage lenders have a rule of thumb—actually, several rules of thumb—that determine how much PITI they feel you are

How Much Can You Afford to Pay?

Monthly Take-Home Pay	25%	30%	35%
$1,000	$250.00	$300.00	$350.00
1,250	312.50	375.00	437.50
1,500	375.00	450.00	525.00
1,750	437.50	525.00	612.50
2,000	500.00	600.00	700.00
2,250	562.50	675.00	787.50
2,500	625.00	750.00	875.00
2,750	687.50	825.00	962.50
3,000	750.00	900.00	1,050.00
3,250	812.50	975.00	1,137.50
3,500	875.00	1,050.00	1,225.00
3,750	937.50	1,125.00	1,312.50
4,000	1,000.00	1,200.00	1,400.00
4,250	1,062.50	1,275.00	1,487.50
4,500	1,125.00	1,350.00	1,575.00
4,750	1,187.50	1,425.00	1,662.50
5,000	1,250.00	1,500.00	1,750.00

capable of handling. In general, lenders do not want you to spend more than 25 to 28 percent of your gross monthly income on PITI (including any homeowner association or condominium fees). In addition, they do not want you to spend more than 30 to 36 percent of your monthly gross income on all installment debt, including your mortgage, credit card payments, car loans, school loans, and the like. The exact amount is up to the individual lender, and has a lot to do with current interest rates. Above is a table that will give you a rough idea about the size of a mortgage payment for which your monthly take-home income will qualify.

Figuring the principal and interest portion of PITI is easy when you consult any of a number of charts and books detailing

THE COST OF BORROWING $1,000

Interest Rate	Monthly Payment
9.00%	$ 8.05
9.50	8.42
10.00	8.78
10.50	9.15
11.00	9.52
11.50	9.90
12.00	10.29
12.50	10.67
13.00	11.06
13.50	11.45
14.00	11.85

monthly payments for almost any size loan for various lengths of time at almost any legal interest rate. Above is a sample, showing monthly payments for borrowing $1,000 at various interest rates for thirty years.

So, for example, to figure the principal and interest on a $44,500 mortgage at 10.5 percent interest, you would multiply 9.150 (from the table) times 44.5 (the number of thousands in $44,500). The answer would be $407.17, the principal and interest portion of the mortgage.

Taxes and insurance are harder to figure, since the amounts differ so much from place to place. A rough estimate is to figure that monthly costs will be one tenth of one percent of the total mortgage. For a $44,500 mortgage, taxes and insurance would run roughly $44.50 a month. (This is a *very* rough estimate.)

Another rough estimate— but a very simple way to "ballpark" these figures— is to assume you'll pay roughly 1 percent of your mortgage each month for PITI— or $445.00 on the $44,500 mortgage. This is most accurate when interest rates are around 10 percent.

A chart detailing monthly payments on thirty-year mortgages up to $200,000 at a variety of interest rates can be found on the facing page.

Monthly Payment Chart

Amount	9%	9.5%	10.0%	10.5%	11.0%	11.5%	12.0%
$30,000	$241	$252	$263	$274	$286	$297	$309
35,000	282	294	307	320	333	347	360
40,000	322	336	351	366	381	396	411
45,000	362	378	395	512	429	446	463
50,000	402	420	439	457	476	495	514
55,000	443	462	483	503	524	545	566
60,000	483	505	527	549	571	594	617
65,000	523	547	570	595	619	644	669
70,000	563	589	614	640	667	693	720
75,000	603	631	658	686	714	743	771
80,000	644	673	702	732	762	792	823
85,000	684	715	746	778	809	842	874
90,000	724	757	790	823	857	891	926
95,000	764	799	834	869	905	941	977
100,000	805	841	878	915	952	990	1,029
110,000	885	925	965	1,006	1,048	1,089	1,132
120,000	966	1,009	1,053	1,098	1,143	1,188	1,234
130,000	1,046	1,093	1,141	1,189	1,238	1,287	1,337
140,000	1,126	1,177	1,229	1,281	1,333	1,386	1,440
150,000	1,207	1,261	1,316	1,372	1,428	1,485	1,543
160,000	1,287	1,345	1,404	1,464	1,524	1,584	1,646
170,000	1,386	1,429	1,492	1,555	1,619	1,684	1,749
180,000	1,448	1,514	1,580	1,647	1,714	1,783	1,852
190,000	1,529	1,598	1,667	1,738	1,809	1,882	1,954
200,000	1,609	1,682	1,755	1,829	1,905	1,981	2,057

Shopping for a Loan

You may be feeling that "I'll be lucky if *anyone* will give me a mortgage," yet that might not be the case. In fact, if you qualify for a mortgage at one lending institution, you'll probably qualify at almost any. But that doesn't mean mortgage lending is so standardized that there's no point in shopping around. In fact, the opposite is true: Although interest rates may be pegged to one standard index or another, lenders' rates, fees, and lending policies vary considerably from lender to lender. So it's important to shop around for the best terms.

You can do a lot of your shopping by phone. By calling several lenders and asking for the terms they are offering on loans, you can begin to learn the range of rates. When you call, ask for a specific loan— say, a $52,500, thirty-year conventional loan on a house for which the selling price is $60,000. Because rates usually differ for 80 percent and 90 percent mortgages, the lender needs to understand your specific financial circumstances (even if they're entirely hypothetical) to give you an accurate quote.

If you've done your homework in previous chapters, you've got a pretty good idea about your personal financial situation. Now, you'll have to make that "pretty good idea" more formal by filling out some reasonably simple but comprehensive statements about your credit history—past, present, and as much into the future as can be seen. Moreover, you'll be asked to verify as much of this information as possible. So, your mortgage application process will be speeded along by your having your financial ducks in a row: proof of your income in the form of paycheck stubs or W-2 statements (the lender will also verify this with your employer); and copies of recent tax returns showing other sources of income, including side-business income or investment and interest income. Other information you should have handy are names and account numbers of outstanding loans—car payments, school loans, and the like— and details about any loans you successfully paid off in recent years. The more such information you have ready and available, the smoother sailing you'll have.

There are several key factors to consider when mortgage shopping:

- ✔ the length, or maturity, of the loan
- ✔ the interest rate
- ✔ the number of points you'll have to pay
- ✔ whether there are application and other fees levied by the lender
- ✔ whether the payments or rates may change
- ✔ how often and how much payments or rates may change
- ✔ whether there is an opportunity for refinancing the loan, if necessary
- ✔ whether the loan can be assumed at the same terms by a subsequent buyer

❑ *Rates and terms.* Interest rates determine the size of your monthly payment. The exact rate you pay is influenced in part by the size of your down payment and the length of the loan term. Generally, the bigger the down payment, the lower the interest rate. If, for example, you make a 10 percent down payment, you can expect an interest rate one-quarter to one-half percent higher than the rate you would pay if you put down 20 percent or more. And rates on a fifteen-year mortgage are usually a bit lower than those on more conventional twenty-year loans, because shorter terms put the lender at less risk.

The interest rate is expressed as an *annual percentage rate,* or APR. This figure includes service charges, points, PMI, and any other costs associated with the loan. Federal law says that at the time you get a loan, you're supposed to get a statement indicating the APR, but there is no law requiring the lender to volunteer the APR when you apply. So you must know enough to ask for it.

❑ *Variable-rate mortgages.* Traditionally, all mortgages were for a fixed term with a fixed interest rate. A $50,000 mortgage at 10 percent interest carried the same monthly fee for all 360 months. More recently, lenders began offering a vast array of adjustable or variable-rate mortgages, in which the interest rate—and the amount of monthly payments—change over time, usually upward. We'll discuss those rates in greater detail later on in this chapter. For now, simply be aware that these types of loans can be very complex, and very difficult to compare from one lender to another. When loan shopping it is critical to get all the details and to make sure you fully understand what you are getting into.

❑ *Closing costs.* At the time of settlement, or closing, you will have to pay a long list of fees—some of them quite nominal, others fairly steep—that are part of the process of buying real estate. The biggest single cost will likely be points. (As stated earlier, one point equals one percent of the amount you borrow.) Points compensate the lender for a variety of costs, and lenders find them a convenient way to receive compensation, especially when interest rates are low, or when you are receiving a below-market FHA or VA loan. So, one of the first questions you'll need to ask after you learn the interest rate is how many points you will have to pay. If it's high—say, three or four points—and you're strapped for cash, you could consider trading lower points for a slightly higher interest rate, but you'll end up paying much more in the long run. Be aware that points are known by a number of terms. Some lenders call them discount fees, others call them loan origination fees.

❑ *Prepayment penalties.* The terms of some mortgages state that if you pay them off early, you must pay a penalty. So, if you have a thirty-year mortgage and decide to sell your house sometime before then, you would be subject to a prepayment penalty when you pay off the balance on the mortgage. If you know that your mortgage contains such a term, you can pass off that penalty to whoever buys your house, but often that terminology is buried amid the fine print. Clearly, the best arrangement is to have no prepayment penalty.

❑ *Assumable mortgages.* An assumable mortgage is one that can be passed on to a new owner at the previous owner's interest rate. For example, if you get an assumable mortgage with a 10 percent interest rate and when you sell your home interest rates are around 12 percent, that assumable mortgage will be a valuable asset; the buyer will save money by assuming your loan and getting a smaller one to pay for the difference between the mortgage balance and the purchase price. Some lenders charge an assumption fee when the mortgage is assumed. When interest rates are low, lenders are reluctant to giving assumable mortgages, but they can be found.

ASKING THE RIGHT QUESTIONS
To sum up, here are some of the questions to ask a lender:

❑ Can I get a lower interest rate by making a bigger down payment?
❑ Do you make FHA or VA loans?
❑ Do you offer variable rate or other alternative mortgages?
❑ What is the best interest rate I can get?

❏ How many points do you charge?
❏ Will you charge fewer points if I pay a higher interest rate?
❏ Is there a prepayment penalty?
❏ Is the loan assumable?
❏ Will I need to pay for private mortgage insurance?
❏ If so, can I shop around for my own PMI?
❏ What is the typical time it takes to process my application?
❏ How long after my application is approved can I go to settlement?

WHERE TO SHOP FOR A MORTGAGE

Nearly every type of financial institution seems to be making mortgages these days, among them:

❏ *Savings and loan associations.* Savings and loans write about half of the single-house and condominium mortgages in the United States. That, in fact, is their principal business. They are also the principal lenders of adjustable-rate mortgages and other alternative mortgages. S&Ls will lend up to 95 percent of a home's appraised value, assuming your income and other factors are in line with their acceptable standards.

❏ *Commercial banks.* These are the second largest mortgage underwriters. They typically require larger down payments than S&Ls— usually, 25 percent or more— and are particularly helpful if you are a long-standing customer. FHA and VA loans require smaller down payments, but many banks refuse to write these loans because of the red tape involved.

❏ *Credit unions.* These are excellent sources of mortgages, although they are often overlooked. Credit unions are nonprofit cooperatives for people employed in the same industry or with some other common bond. Some 58 million Americans belong to a credit union. Because they are nonprofit organizations, they can offer lower down payment requirements, lower interest rates, and lower closing costs. They are also a good source of second mortgages. If you belong to a credit union, begin your shopping there. Not all credit unions offer mortgages, however, and most that do offer a limited assortment of types.

❏ *Mutual savings banks.* These are similar to savings and loan associations and exist in seventeen states: Alaska, Connecticut, Delaware, Indiana, Maine, Maryland, Massachusetts, Minnesota, New Hampshire, New Jersey, New York, Oregon, Pennsylvania, Rhode Island, Vermont, Washington, and Wisconsin. Mutual savings banks are run for the mutual benefit of their depositors, and they invest most of their assets in mortgages.

❏ *Mortgage banks.* Despite their name, these "banks" don't accept deposits. These are financing companies that offer mortgages, which they in turn sell to large institutional investors such as pension-fund and life insurance companies. The country's two principal mortgage banks are sponsored by the federal government: the Federal National Mortgage Association (commonly referred to as "Fannie Mae") and the Federal Home Loan Mortgage Corporation ("Freddie Mac"). Both of these were established to help funnel investors' money— including foreign investors— into the U.S. mortgage market. Most of these offer only fixed-rate mortgages. Many mortgage bankers work with real estate agents, who get commissions for the loans they refer.

❏ *Mortgage brokers.* These individuals and organizations don't offer mortgages themselves. Instead, they locate the best loan available and serve as an intermediary between you and the lender. Most mortgage brokers are compensated by the lender, so they don't charge for their services, although a few will try to receive compensation at both ends. You should never pay more for a mortgage acquired through a broker than you would if you dealt directly with the lender. Also be aware of the fact that not all brokers are independent; some are subsidiaries of a specific lender and route all their business to one source. In effect, they are simply a marketing arm of a lender. And a few mortgage brokers have been known to offer "bait-and-switch" tactics: They lure you in with the promise of a mortgage with very attractive terms, then at the last minute inform you that the loan was no longer available, hoping that you'll agree to whatever loan they can come up with. One good approach is to use a recommended mortgage broker but to continue loan shopping on your own to see if you can come up with better terms yourself.

If a realty agent offers to serve as your broker, beware: under federal law, it is illegal for agents to receive fees, kickbacks, or "anything of value" in exchange for referrals.

❑ *Builders and developers.* New-home builders usually reserve large sums of money at local lending institutions and make them available to their clients. They aren't making loans themselves; they are simply acting as middlemen. Because the builder is bringing a bulk of business to the lender, the terms may be quite attractive, but this is not always the case. Again, you will be best served by shopping around yourself to compare the builders' terms with what you can find yourself.

❑ *Other sources.* You may want to check any of the following as sources for mortgage money:

- ✔ pension funds
- ✔ labor unions
- ✔ fraternal organizations
- ✔ state housing finance authorities
- ✔ local mortgage revenue bond programs
- ✔ insurance companies
- ✔ the company where you work

JUDGING THE ANSWERS

There are three essential characteristics of a good lender, and with a bit of luck and some shopping around, you'll have the luxury of choosing the one that best meets these criteria:

❑ Loans should be processed locally, rather than being shipped out of town to some faceless committee.
❑ Loan officers should be knowledgeable and able to explain terms and conditions in plain English.
❑ Loans should be timely and at the terms promised.

By talking with one or more real estate agents or attorneys, and by talking face-to-face with the lenders themselves, you should be able to unearth which lender is right for you.

To help keep track of the various terms and rates offered by each prospective lender, you might want to create a simple comparison chart to make sure your comparing all terms equally.

In Chapter 6, we'll deal with the process of applying for a mortgage, as well as with the growing types of mortgages you might want to consider.

Chapter 5
Wheeling and Dealing

You can use all the help you can get when it comes time to wheel and deal on a house. This is no task for the fainthearted. We're talking about tens of thousands of dollars—perhaps a hundred thousand or more. Having some good help on hand may save you far more than it will cost in professional fees.

Remember that if you are being represented by a real estate agent—unless it is someone who is working for you and receiving compensation directly from you and not the seller— that agent is *not* your ally. He or she is being paid a commission by the *seller* of the property, so the more money you pay, the more money the agent will receive. The agent, however helpful he or she may be, is not necessarily on your side. (On the practical level, the agent does know how to negotiate between buyer and seller to ensure that the sale doesn't slip away, and this can be helpful indeed, but not the same as having someone specifically representing your interest. And even though the agent is paid by the seller, the agent receives no commission if no sale is consummated, so a good agent will be equally interested in negotiating between buyer and seller than in getting the highest price for the seller.)

Consider hiring a lawyer. You may shudder at the mere thought of engaging such a professional—lawyers don't, after all, have the highest level of our society's trust—but it may well be worth the few hundred dollars it will cost you. Most lawyers are adept at sorting through the seemingly endless array of fine-print forms you must go through when buying real estate. Most are also skilled negotiators, something most of us lay people aren't particularly good at. And the same attorney who will help you through negotiations can also hold your hand through closing.

Be wary of an attorney provided by the real estate agent handling the sale. The agent may suggest that the lawyer will answer questions and help you sort through the legal mumbo-jumbo at closing, but if the lawyer is being paid for by the agent (who is paid for by the seller), you will *not* be getting the representation you need. Some lawyers who work with realty agents have direct ties to lenders, title insurance companies, or others who may be involved in the transaction. Again, you want to find someone who will work just for *you*.

As with finding a lender, your search for a lawyer may begin with a bank, with the agent (yes, the agent may recommend someone, as long as the agent isn't paying the lawyer's fee), friends, your employer, or the local bar association. When you first call the lawyer to make an appointment, there are several things you should ask:

❑ What services will you provide, and at what fee (ideally broken down by service)?
❑ Do you have any ties with lenders, title insurance companies, or the seller?
❑ What experience do you have in real estate?
❑ Will you negotiate with the seller on my behalf?
❑ Will you attend the closing?

BUYERS' BROKERS

One fast-growing trend in real estate is the use of a "buyer's broker." As the name implies, this is a broker who represents you, the buyer, as opposed to the listing agent, who represents the seller. In fact, more than a few large realty companies have opened divisions devoted exclusively to representing buyers.

Much like a lawyer, a buyer's broker will help you negotiate the price and terms of a property, as well as pointing out both the strengths and weaknesses of properties you are considering. The buyer's broker splits the commission with the listing agent. At least, that's the theory. In some cases, listing agents or sellers have refused to split the commission, causing the buyer to pay the fee. In a few cases, real estate agents have imposed obstacles to sales, such as blocking buyers' brokers from viewing homes, or obstructing them in efforts to present purchase offers. In a seller's market, in which several people may be vying for the same property, a buyer's broker could cause enough delay as to make you lose the sale.

Clearly, this is a new and rather controversial aspect of the home-buying process. While the idea of a buyer's broker makes perfect sense, you should tread this new ground carefully, perhaps checking around to learn the local climate toward buyers' brokers, before plunging in.

Making an Offer

Conventional wisdom is that sellers always ask more for their property than they expect to get, so that there is always room to lower the price. As with most conventional wisdom, it often *isn't* true. A significant number of sellers really know what their home is worth and list it at a price, including the word "firm." You can either pay their price or look elsewhere. And many homes truly are excellent buys even at their full asking prices.

Firm prices are particularly common during a seller's market, in which there are more buyers than sellers, and in certain real estate markets or particularly desirable neighborhoods, where affordable housing is at a premium. In some areas, in fact, housing prices often sell *above* their asking price, as two or more would-be buyers bid each other up. Clearly, for these buyers, the specific house or location is more important than getting the lowest price.

But even many of these "firm" prices aren't as firm as you'd think, and there are other considerations beyond selling price that can make the purchase terms more favorable to you; more about those in a moment. The fact is, most homes sell for between 5 percent and 10 percent below their asking price, and whether you are being represented by a broker, lawyer, or yourself, the process of getting to that price doesn't vary much.

Getting the Facts

Before making an offer, you should do some homework. First and foremost, you must know the house—its good points and bad points. Go over your inspection checklist and list the problem areas; these will be among your key negotiating points. Have a realistic idea of how much it will cost to fix the problems, and to renovate and redecorate things to your satisfaction. Ideally, you will be able to purchase the property for at least that amount of money below the asking price.

You will also be well served by having a list of "comparables." These are examples of recent sales prices of comparable homes within a mile of the house you are considering; the closer they are to your potential new home, the better. A "comparable" house needn't be exactly like yours, but it should have roughly the same size and number of bedrooms, and be about the same age, give or take a few years. Keep in mind that some seemingly identical houses a few blocks away may be worth different amounts due to a variety of factors, from the type of construction to the availability of on-street parking. To make the comparisons among different properties meaningful, it may be helpful to translate the sales prices into dollars per square foot. For example, a 1,450-square-foot house that sold for $80,000 cost $55.17 per square foot ($80,000 divided by 1,450). It would also be helpful to know the difference between their listing prices and actual sales prices; a real estate agent may have this information handy.

THE OFFER TO BUY

The offer to buy is a formal process with specific rules that must be followed. It is not like buying a used car, in which two parties sit in the seller's living room or talk on the phone and casually make offers and counteroffers. In real estate, the offer—usually known as an "offer to purchase" or a "purchase agreement"—is made in writing. It is a formal document, signed and dated, and is a legally binding contract that states how much you will pay for the house, provided certain conditions are met. Because it is a legal instrument, your agent or lawyer should review the offer before it is presented to the seller (or soon thereafter; some states have a three- to-five-day grace period during which a lawyer will be able to review an offer to buy and make any appropriate changes in it).

The offer should have a time limit—a couple of days in which the seller must accept or reject it. Some sellers or their agents will ask for more time, but think twice about granting it unless there is good reason to do so. Many agents and sellers like as much time as possible to "shop" your offer around. For example: "I've been offered $75,000. If you make it $78,000, it's yours." At the very least, you should insist on having the right to top any other offer the seller receives, assuming it makes sense to do so.

If you are working with an agent, he or she will present the offer, usually in person. You can revoke your offer at any time until the seller accepts it. If the seller rejects your offer, it cannot later be accepted unless it is rewritten and formally resubmitted. When you sign the offer, you must also put down some "earnest money," indicating that you are serious about all this. The amount varies, usually at least $1,000, perhaps pegged at 1 or 2 percent of the sale price. The money will be placed in escrow, to be applied toward the purchase price at settlement, or returned to you if the deal falls through.

In addition to accepting or rejecting your offer, the seller has a third option: a counteroffer. You, then, can accept, reject, or counter the seller's counteroffer, with offers going back and forth until there is a resolution either way. All of this happens fairly rapidly, most likely in a few days. Usually, both you and the seller are anxious to resolve things—the seller doesn't want you to have a change of heart; you want to know whether or not to keep looking—so it isn't in anyone's interest to sit on an offer or counteroffer for very long. It's important to keep things on a pleasant and reasonable level, because even after both parties accept the offer, there's still plenty to negotiate.

Negotiating price is a delicate matter. There are no rules of thumb for how much to offer below the sales price, although it is extremely rare that a house sell for 20 percent or more less than the asking price. Coming up with the opening offer is more art than science, and a great deal of its success depends on plain old luck. For example, if no one else is bidding on a property and the buyer is anxious to sell it, or if someone who outbids you is unable to secure financing or meet other conditions, your offer may be accepted. As you can see, there is a lot here that is out of your control.

You can never tell how a seller will react to your initial offer. It may be that the seller is aware that the asking price is bloated, and already is expecting to get less for it, so your offer may be in the right range. It may be that the owner needs to sell it fast, and will accept the first offer within reason. It may be that there are no other offers. Or the seller may want to hang in there and wait for someone to come closer to the asking price. Having a professional working on your side will help reduce the second guessing, and will increase the chances your offer will be accepted.

By the way, don't be afraid to make a purchase offer on a house you really want that is already sold but not settled. For a variety of reasons, not all offers go through. By being the "back-up buyer," you will be the first in line if the original deal falls through.

TERMS OF SALE

Price negotiations were the easy part: There was only one matter to agree on. Now it's time to negotiate the terms of sale, including a host of details you probably haven't thought much about. All must be included in the original offer to buy. Among other details, this document will state:

❏ the price of the property
❏ what's included in the sale (house, land, fixtures, etc.)
❏ the date of sale (the "closing") and when you can move in
❏ the contingencies—under what conditions you can get out of
   the agreement

Purchase agreements vary widely from city to city and state to state, so having a lawyer will be helpful. Unless required by state law, be wary of anything called a "standard" purchase agreement, because there is no such thing. (In some states—California, for example—most real estate agents use a standardized "Real Estate Purchase Contract and Receipt for Deposit" prepared by the California Association of Realtors, but it is not required that this form be used.) Don't accept anyone's claim that "I can't change this because it's already printed on the form." Even if something is neatly and professionally printed on paper, it can be modified or deleted, as long as both parties agree and initial the change.

Let's examine the key components of the basic purchase agreement.

❏ *Earnest money*. When you sign the purchase agreement, you will probably have to make a deposit on the house. This is called "earnest money." It is a token cash amount—usually $500 to $1,000—that binds you and the seller to the terms of the agreement. In some cases, deposits can be as little as $100. The money will be held by the broker, the seller's lawyer, or some other third party. While this money is refundable if the deal doesn't go through, it is in your interest to put down as little as possible in earnest money, in case complications arise that slow down the refund. However, the earnest money will not be refunded if you back out of the sale for reasons not provided for in the agreement.

❏ *Price and terms*. The purchase agreement will state the price, and whether it will be "all cash"—that is, paid in full at the time of closing—or whether there will be any other financing arrangements. (More on seller financing in Chapter 6.)

❏ *The particulars*. This includes a legal description of the property, the expiration date of the offer, and the date of closing and occupancy.

❏ *Contingencies*. As stated earlier, these can be many and varied, depending on any unique aspects of the deal. The following are the most common:

> 1. A *financing contingency* indicates that the contract depends on your ability to obtain a mortgage or other financing within a given period of time—say, thirty to forty-five days—and at a stated interest rate and length of term. Such a clause might read: "This purchase offer is contingent upon buyer and the property qualifying within thirty days for a new first mortgage of at least $60,000 at a fixed interest rate not exceeding 10.5 percent for a term of thirty years and a loan fee not exceeding two points." So, if you can't get the money at the terms you want, the deal's off and your deposit will be refunded.

> 2. *Inspection contingencies* indicate that the deal hinges on your having inspections done on the house to your

satisfaction for such things as termites and other pests, radon, the electrical system, plumbing, the structure, and the appliances. The contingency must state the time period within which the inspections are to be completed. The contingency may state that the contract will become null and void if the inspections reveal certain conditions, such as termites, unsafe aluminum wiring, asbestos insulation, or other potential hazards or defects. Or, these problems could result in credits to you from the seller toward the purchase price, roughly equivalent to the amount it would take to remedy the problems, or the approximate value they detract from the property. In effect, you'd be reducing the purchase price.

3. An *appraisal contingency* states that the offer may be withdrawn if the house is not appraised for at least a specific amount. This may be particularly important in getting a VA- or FHA-insured loan.

4. *Sale of your house contingency* states that if you are unable to sell your existing home within a given time period, the purchase agreement becomes null and void.

❏ *Agreement of condition.* This will ensure that the property on which you make an offer on is the same property you'll get, and that there are no hidden defects about which the seller hasn't told you. For example: "Seller represents that all defects in this property known to the seller have been disclosed to the buyer in writing." You should also state that the offer is contingent "upon buyer obtaining a satisfactory inspection report on the property from a professional property inspector of buyer's choice at buyer's expense within five business days." You probably should further state that on settlement, the property will be in the same condition as it is on the date of the offer, ordinary and reasonable wear and tear notwithstanding; also that the seller will keep the property insured to an amount equal to the sales price until settlement. (You may also consider protecting your interests by asking your insurance agent for a binder on the new property during this period. The price will be minimal.) In some jurisdictions, there is a legally required disclosure statement that must be filled out by the seller, indicating any significant defects or malfunctions in any of the property's major components.

❏ *Completion of work.* If any work is being done on the house by the seller, the contract should indicate that the work must be completed prior to settlement. Clearly, this is a crucial condition when buying a newly built home.

❏ *What's included in the sale.* The contract should include an inventory of items that both you and the seller agree are part of the deal. Aside from the house itself, these items may include appliances, lighting fixtures, carpets, mirrors, patio furniture, tools, supplies, and anything else that isn't physically attached to the house. Don't assume that something will be there when you move in unless you specifically state it in the contract.

❏ *Vacate or rent.* If the seller doesn't move out of the house in time for you to take possession, the seller should agree to pay your living expenses for the period in which you must find other arrangements. Alternatively, upon settlement the sellers could become tenants in your new house and pay you rent during their stay. If either of these conditions suits you, it should be so stated.

❏ *Taxes and utilities.* Property tax bills arrive once or twice a year, so it's possible that the seller will have prepaid some of the property taxes for the period following settlement. If so, there may be a stipulation that you will reimburse the seller at settlement for the prepaid taxes. The same may be true for utilities: If the seller just filled an oil or propane tank, and that fuel will convey to the buyer, the buyer may have to pay for it.

❏ *Title.* "Title" in real estate refers to legal ownership, the way it is recorded in public records. When someone borrows money and puts up his or her home for collateral, that is usually recorded on the official title. Other legal proceedings, from contracts to bankruptcies to lawsuits, also can place a cloud on the title. The title records are the final determinant of ownership of property, and it is important that the title to a house you are buying be free and clear.

In the purchase agreement, the seller must warrant—that is, promise or prove—that he or she will deliver at settlement a marketable title, one that is free and clear of all liens and encumbrances except those which you specifically agree to in the contract or approve when the results of the title search are reported to you. You may negotiate as to who will pay for the title search service to determine whether the title is clear. Before a property transfer can take place legally, a title search must be conducted to determine that the seller has the legal right to transfer title to a new owner. In addition, you can purchase title insurance that will protect you if something later emerges to place a cloud on the title. (The lender of your mortgage will likely require you to purchase title insurance, but this only protects the lender, not you, in the event of problems. You may be able to save some money by purchasing two title insurance policies—one covering the lender, another covering you—simultaneously.) Ideally, because the seller is guaranteeing the title, he or she should bear the cost of title search insurance. If the seller won't bear the cost, or even share it, you are strongly urged to obtain title insurance at your own expense. The expense—typically between $100 and $250—is well worth it, considering the risks you will be taking by not being covered.

❏ *Closing costs.* Some of those costs already have been described: loan charges and title insurance, for example. There are several other costs, which we'll get into in Chapter 4. For purposes of the purchase agreement you must spell out which party—buyer or seller—will pay which costs. There really is no standard way of divvying up the closing-costs pie; everything is negotiable, and here is where a broker or lawyer representing you can save you some money.

❏ *Seller default.* This clause states that if the seller changes his or her mind and backs out of the sale, the seller must pay you an amount equal to or double the amount of your deposit. Clearly, it is in your interest to give the seller as much disincentive as possible to back out. If the seller simply gives you your money back, suffering no financial damage in the process, there will be a greater chance that the deal will fall through.

Of course, the seller may well want to add a *buyer default* clause, stating that if you back out, the seller may sue you for damages, up to and including the full purchase price of the house. You should delete any such provisions, limiting your liability to your earnest money or down payment.

❑ *Arbitration clause*. Sometimes, problems arise before, during, or after settlement that can't easily be negotiated between the buyer and seller, and for which neither party wants to file an expensive and time-consuming lawsuit. One common alternative is to provide for binding arbitration by the American Arbitration Association, which provides skilled arbitrators to help work out equitable solutions; because its decisions are binding, you are agreeing to abide by the outcome of the arbitration. The clause probably should state that the buyer and seller will share equally the cost of the arbitration, which may run to several hundred dollars.

❑ *Signatures*. Make sure that all present owners sign the purchase agreement. If both a husband and wife own a property, or if there are several owners, or if a parent co-signed a child's mortgage and the lender placed title in both's name, each individual should sign this agreement.

Look over the purchase agreement carefully. It plots the course for all that is to follow in the home-buying process, and a few key phrases—whether included or omitted—can make all the difference. Keep in mind that there are many points of negotiation involved in the purchase agreement, the results of which can cost or save you hundreds or thousands of dollars. Don't sign the purchase agreement until both you and the seller agree on all the terms.

In the next chapter, we'll go through the process of applying for a mortgage, and also take a look at the seemingly endless array of mortgages.

Chapter 6
Getting a Mortgage

One of the first things you'll need to do when you make an offer on a house is to apply for a mortgage. As you learned in Chapter 4, the better prepared you are when you approach a lender for a mortgage, the better your chances for success.

When you apply, you'll need the following items:

❑ a copy of the sales contract
❑ a blank check
❑ the house location survey.

The mortgage application is a fairly standard document, due largely to federal laws that ban discrimination and require lenders to be very careful in the way they ask applicants questions. Indeed, the lender can legally ask you only the questions on the application; they can't dig into your personal life. Although not all do, lenders are supposed to gather "just the facts," not pass judgment on you. Still, despite years of civil rights acts and antidiscrimination laws, there is ample proof that some lenders do have a bias against minorities, women, and people living in certain neighborhoods, regardless of their financial condition, credit records, or other qualifications.

Along with the application, you'll also be asked to pay a processing fee, typically around $100. (The fee may be waived when buying a home in a new development, in which the builder may have negotiated a package deal with the lender that foregoes this fee.) The processing fee is nonrefundable: If you're turned down, you won't get your money back. You may also be asked at this time to pay for a credit check ($15 to $25) and an appraisal ($100 to $250); again, this money will be nonrefundable.

When you submit the application, you'll receive a statement from the lender giving an estimate of the closing costs, along with a booklet explaining settlement. The lender is required by law to give you these, although they are only good-faith estimates. You may want to ask the lender how much higher than these estimates your actual costs might be; there probably is no reason that the lender shouldn't be able to provide a reasonably close estimate.

Among the information you'll have to provide:

❑ *Employment income.* There are two important considerations: how much you make, and how long you've been making it. Also important is how often you change jobs; lenders favor stable applicants who don't bring a lot of uncertainty to the table. Only the past two or three years' worth of job history is relevant, although you might be asked to provide salaries and employer names and addresses as far as five or ten years back. Old tax returns will be one good source of information, because they show exactly how much you made (at least for tax purposes) each year. Also helpful are old pay stubs, if you've kept them.

Past employment is one thing. Also important is how much you'll make in the *future.* Are you in line for a fat raise or a promotion? Do you get a raise every six months like clockwork? Let that be known.

Self-employed people often face obstacles, although they can easily be overcome. Two or three years' worth of tax returns are usually sufficient proof of income, although the type of work you do may be considered as well in discerning your financial stability and future prospects. If your business is incorporated, you'll have to provide corporate tax returns as well. Self-employed applicants may be scrutinized extra-carefully unless their businesses are long established and their income rock-solid.

❑ *Household income.* Of course, if the mortgage is being applied for by two people, both individuals' job income counts, as do other types of compensation: bonuses, part time work, alimony, retirement income, parental support, investment income, rental income, stock dividends, and child support and maintenance payments; you should be able to show that alimony and child-support payments come on a reliable basis.

❑ *Equity*. As stated earlier, lenders like to make loans to applicants who have a substantial investment in their property in the form of a healthy down payment—20 percent or more. Lenders frown on money borrowed for the down payment or closing costs, figuring that by taking on so many debts, applicants will be biting off more than they can chew, financially speaking. Gifts from family members (or anyone else) probably won't decrease your desirability. However, you likely will be asked to get a letter from your benefactor confirming that the money need not be repaid. If you are putting down a relatively modest down payment, you may be asked to prove that you have the money available to cover the down payment and closing costs; you can be prepared by bringing in copies of bank statements or passbooks.

❑ *Other assets*. The lender will want to examine other aspects of your financial picture, including other investments you may have, particularly real estate. If you have a cash-value life insurance policy, find out the surrender value (as opposed to the face value) of the policy. Let the lender know if you possess one or more automobiles that are fully paid for. Bring statements, canceled checks, or other documents that will confirm the amount and nature of these investments.

❑ *Debts and liabilities*. These, of course, are the other side of the financial picture. After all, your income may be up there in the stratosphere, but if your monthly credit card bills, installment loans, car payments, and tuition loans eat up the lion's share, you'll have a difficult time proving your credit worthiness. Among the things that will be considered under this category are loans and notes, other mortgages, insurance premiums of all types, alimony, child support, and medical bills. Please understand: There's nothing wrong with having debts. (Indeed, lenders like to know that an applicant has a reliable history of making debt payments on a timely basis.) It's simply that the amount of debt you have relative to the size of your income will be an important factor in the lender's eyes.

❑ *Credit history*. Your history of handling debts in the past is looked at carefully by lenders. If your credit history isn't exactly sterling—if you regularly miss payments or make them late, for example—you're going to have a tough time convincing a lender to lend you tens of thousands of dollars. (Would *you* lend someone tens of thousands of dollars if they didn't have a good history paying bills?) Serious matters like bankruptcy set off particularly loud warning bells. Still, federal law says that you have the chance to explain these matters to a prospective creditor. And if any of the information is incorrect, you have the opportunity to refute and correct it. Sometimes, a problem on your record results more from circumstances (an illness, a layoff, a sick child, etc.) than from bad payment habits. A letter of explanation may ease the concern of those examining your record. If you're concerned about your credit record, you're advised to examine it before you apply. Ask a banker or real estate agent which credit reporting agencies are most commonly used in your area, then give them a call (they're listed in the Yellow Pages under "Credit Reporting Agencies") to find out the procedures and cost of getting a copy of your credit record. It will set you back $10 or $20.

If you don't have a credit record on file, you should start one immediately. Apply for a credit card from a local department store or gas station. Also easy to get is a check-overdraft account at a local bank, assuming you've had the same address and job for six months or more. By doing so, your name will be entered into the files of one or more local credit reporting agencies. But it can take months for your name to work its way through the system, and even then your record won't show a long, reliable history.

To facilitate an examination of your credit, you should be prepared to provide the lender with your Social Security number, names and addresses of your past and present residences and employers, the account numbers of your major credit cards, and information on any outstanding loans, checking overdraft lines of credit and the like.

When all this information is gathered and documented, the lender will check you out. There will be a credit report and a call to your employer to verify your employment. There will be an appraisal made of the home, to determine its value relative to the mortgage your are seeking. Lenders want to know that if you default on your mortgage, they'll be able to sell the house for enough money to pay off the mortgage and to cover some additional legal costs. These appraisals are an inexact science at best, and are superficial compared to a professional home inspection; in some cases, the appraiser will merely drive by the house, perhaps not even going inside, sometimes scarcely slowing down. The house is then compared to other properties within the radius of a mile to see if the price is comparable for similar houses. If the mortgage represents too great a percentage of the value of the house, your application may be turned down. To remedy this, you'd have to make a bigger down payment. However, you might consider hiring your own appraiser to look at the house; if your appraisal is substantially more than the lender's you should submit it as a counterappraisal.

APPROVAL OR REJECTION?

The results of all this information-gathering will be sent to a loan committee, a group of officers of the lender's organization who pass judgment on all applications; they usually meet once a week, although the frequency will depend on the amount of applications being considered at any one time. The overall decision-making process can take two weeks or more, although, as stated at the beginning of Chapter 4, several competitive organizations are trying to cut that time down to a few days—or even a few hours.

You may be surprised to learn that some lenders grade their applicants much the way you were graded in high school: as an A, B, or C risk. The A risks are those with impeccable credit histories and financial statements. Their approval is fast and certain, and at a more favorable interest rate—as much as three or four points lower than the B and C applicants. The B applicants have a fairly regular record of slow or late payments and less-substantial assets (or more-substantial debts). They will probably need a 25 percent or higher down payment for mortgage approval. The C candidates have more serious blemishes on their records, such as a bankruptcy or being behind on their installment debts for a period of 30 days or more, or four months behind on a revolving charge account such as Visa or department store charge cards. They may still qualify for a mortgage, but probably not without a 30 to 35 percent down payment and a loan at a considerably higher interest rate.

If your application is accepted, you'll be granted a loan commitment for a given period of time, usually sixty days, at a fixed rate of interest. Unless you are buying from a builder who already has secured a chunk of mortgage money at a fixed interest rate to lure buyers, this is the first time you'll know what your actual interest rate will be. (The rate in effect at the time you apply for a loan is not the applicable one; you're charged the rate in effect at the time your loan is approved. During times of fast-changing interest rates, this can be quite disconcerting if your application is delayed for any purpose.) If you can't go to settlement on your purchase within the loan commitment period, you usually can apply for an extension, although not necessarily at the same interest rate. So the date of loan commitment begins a ticking clock against which you must race in order to close the deal before your money disappears. And more than one deal has disappeared because a loan wasn't able to be approved in time.

What should you do if you're rejected? It happens. Not everyone gets a mortgage. But some people are turned down who shouldn't be. If you are turned down for any loan, the lender is required by federal law to give you a statement explaining the reason for turning you down. The lender must reveal the source of information about you that was consulted, such as the name of the local credit bureau that provided information about your record. Under the Fair Credit Reporting Act, you have the right to request the specific information leading to denial; you must do this within sixty days of the rejection. You also have the right to correct any false or misleading information and to have your application reconsidered based on the amended information.

Of course, there may have been one or more logical reasons for your being turned down, such as insufficient income or too many other debts. If so, don't panic: there are other options. You can search for a loan from a lender with less-restrictive policies, although probably at a higher interest rate. You can scrape up some money for a larger down payment, meaning you won't have to qualify for as large a loan. And there are a host of other creative options, which we'll get into in a moment. But first, here's a quick overview of the types of mortgages on the market, and some of the advantages and disadvantages of each.

Types of Mortgages

There are dozens of types of mortgages available these days, with new ones cropping up every few months. In general, they fall into two basic categories: conventional mortgages and so-called alternative mortgages.

CONVENTIONAL MORTGAGES
These are the workhorses of the mortgage industry: thirty-year, fixed-rate loans, meaning the interest rate won't change over the life of the mortgage. They are sometimes known by the acronym FRM, for "fixed-rate mortgage." Until a few years ago, when high interest rates led lenders to become more creative to entice borrowers, they were virtually the only type of mortgage available. Among their advantages are their certainty: You'll never have to guess how much your mortgage payments will be a few years down the road (changes in taxes and insurance can raise the PITI over the course of the loan; the principal and interest portions remain constant, however). If you're lucky enough to get one of these mortgages when interest rates are low—say, at 10 percent or below— you'll be buffeted against major surges in the financial marketplace. However, fixed-rate mortgages aren't as readily available as they once were, especially during times of low rates. Because rates these days change so much and so quickly, lenders aren't particularly keen on locking themselves into long-term loans that can't be changed as market conditions warrant. In other words, availability depends a lot on market conditions.

But even conventional mortgages aren't quite so standard anymore. Whereas the thirty-year mortgage has been the norm among FRMs, there are now fifteen-year and even forty-year mortgages available. But you should hesitate taking a mortgage shorter than thirty years. A better strategy would be to take a thirty-year mortgage but pretend that it was a fifteen-year mortgage, making an extra *principal* payment each month. This will be less money than it seems: The bulk of mortgage payments, especially during the first ten years, is substantially interest; a $500 mortgage payment might include only $40 or $50 worth of payments on the principal. By doing this, if you run into financial problems, you can still fall back into the payment schedule of your thirty-year mortgage. If you lock yourself into the higher payment schedule of a fifteen-year mortgage, you won't have the luxury of this choice. As for forty-year mortgages, they make sense only when their (slightly) lower monthly payments mean the difference between qualifying and not qualifying for the loan.

ADJUSTABLE-RATE MORTGAGES

Once upon a time, you could get a mortgage for between 8 and 10 percent and put your money in a savings account paying 5 or 6 percent. That worked well for lenders, borrowers, and savers— as long as interest rates remained stable and low. But in the late 1970s and early 1980s, a time in which interest rates were rising rapidly and banking services were being deregulated, all of this got turned on its head. If you were lucky, you could get an 8 percent mortgage one day, and a few months later earn 9 or 10 percent on your savings account. And with double-digit inflation taken into account, you were in effect getting an interest-free mortgage. Clearly, this placed lenders under considerable risk, and some changes were in order.

The result was the advent of adjustable-rate mortgages, known as ARMs (they are also known as variable-rate mortgages, among several other names), which allow lenders to adapt to changing conditions and reduce their risk. With an ARM, the interest rate fluctuates over the course of the loan, going up and down in tandem with other interest rates every year or so. That shortens the time for which lenders must commit themselves to a specific interest rate; the more frequently lenders can adjust their rates, the lower their risk—and the greater yours. Yet many of these loans actually lower monthly payments, at least in early years, making them particularly attractive to first-time home buyers. The bad news, of course, is that payments in later years may rise to unbearable levels.

Who should get an ARM? It depends in part on your personal circumstances, your best guess about future interest rates, and on the specific terms of the mortgage itself. Let's take a look at the basic types of alternative mortgages.

As the name suggests, the interest rate on ARMs is flexible. If interest rates go up, so does the rate on the mortgage, along with the monthly payments. If they go down, the interest rates and monthly payments follow accordingly. While there are many variations on this theme, the interest rate on most ARMs is tied to an index—say, one and a half percentage points above the one-year Treasury bill rate. Other common indexes include three-year Treasury issues, five-year Treasury issues, and the Federal Home Loan Bank Board Series of Closed Loans. So, for example, if the current one-year T-bill rate is 8.5 percent, the ARM rate might be 10 percent. But not all lenders use the same index or the same number of percentage points above a particular index number. Most ARM interest rates are adjusted annually or every three years; some ARMs are adjusted every five years.

One big advantage of ARMs is that the initial interest rate is usually lower than that of conventional mortgages, because lenders aren't taking as big a risk as they do when they establish a fixed interest rate for a thirty-year period. A lower interest rate means lower monthly payments, meaning in turn that you can buy more house with less money. For some people with tight budgets, the money saved with an ARM could mean the difference between qualifying and not qualifying for a loan.

But it doesn't take a math whiz to see that there is one big potential problem here: What happens if interest rates zoom into the stratosphere, as they did in the late 1970s, when the prime rate, which major banks charge their best customers, was near 20 percent? Clearly, a mortgage that paralleled such a meteoric rise could result in a lot of people no longer being able to afford their monthly payments. Most ARMs come with some restrictions or "caps" that protect borrowers against these kinds of enormous rate hikes. For example, a loan might have a 2-percent-per-year cap, meaning that the interest rate can't go up more than 2 percent a year. (It could go *down* more than 2 percent a year if interest rates plunged; most ARMs have no limit on how far rates can drop.) ARMs may have provisions that fix the initial interest rate for, say, the first two years; this would be desirable, of course.

Some ARMs can be converted within the first few years into fixed-rate mortgages at a market interest rate at the time of conversion. A one-time conversion fee will likely be charged. "Convertibles" were introduced in the early 1980s, primarily to sell ARMs to a reluctant public. But they may offer the best of both worlds—allowing the first-time buyer to get the low interest rate of an ARM, then getting the security of the fixed rate after a few years. An ARM may be ideal if you're planning on selling your house after only a few years: You can take advantage of the lower rate offered by ARMs interest the first few years, paying off the mortgage when you sell the house—before the rates have much time to rise.

But with ARMs, the down side is always there: National or international financial matters can send rates on an upward spiral, rising 50 percent or more in just a few years. In that sense, ARMs are a risky way to go, giving you less control over the way you manage your money. For example, if the rate were to keep rising the maximum 2 percent for several years, your mortgage would be 10 percentage points higher after five years. On a $50,000, thirty-year mortgage with a beginning interest rate of 10 percent, that would mean that monthly payments would jump from $438.79 to $835.51—an extra $4,760.64 a year for interest alone!

When comparing ARMs, it's important to look at the loan index and the lender's margin. As stated earlier, many lenders base their ARM interest rates on Treasury issues. The trouble with that index, however, is that it is relatively volatile, going up and down every few weeks or months. A less volatile index—one that will give you smoother ups and downs—is one based on the actual cost of money the lender is paying, known as the cost-of-funds index. The lender's margin represents the difference between the index and the interest rate you actually pay. It is usually two percentage points, but some lenders charge two and a half or three percent. Shop around for a loan with a margin as close to two percent as possible.

In fact, there's a phenomenon called negative amortization that can occur with some adjustable-rate mortgages. Some ARMs are designed to help borrowers by keeping monthly payments the same for the life of the loan. What's adjustable in these arrangements is the principal—the amount you borrow. So, if interest rates were to rise, the extra interest—the difference between what you pay and what you should pay with the new interest rate—would be added to your mortgage balance. The good news is that this keeps your cash-flow even. The bad news is that during a time of rising rates, your principal could rise enough so that *you end up owing more than you borrowed*. Fortunately, most ARMs aren't based on a negative amortization schedule. But some are.

The bottom line is that you must shop hard for an ARM you can live with. You have to be on guard: there are more hidden costs and unknowns than with conventional mortgages and various rates, fees, and terms that may be rather complex. You'll do best by consulting an expert—preferably not the lender who can consider your unique circumstances dispassionately.

To sum up, here are some tips on shopping for an adjustable-rate mortgage:

❏ Check the interest rates for conventional mortgages. If they're low, give second thoughts to going with an ARM.
❏ Look at more than just the initial interest rate of an ARM. Look at the number of points charged, the index used, the lender's margin, the annual and lifetime caps in interest rate rises, and any extra fees. To truly grasp the cost of a particular ARM, you'll have to evaluate and compare a bundle of interrelated costs.
❏ Have an expert examine all the fine print that may contain clauses that will come back to haunt you later on.
❏ When comparing loans, determine which loan will hurt you the least when interest rates zoom up.
❏ Make sure the loan has a tight cap—for example, no more than 2 percent annually, or 5 percent over the life of the loan.
❏ Make sure there is no *minimum* interest rate, in the event that rates in general take a plunge.
❏ Find out if the ARM is based on a negative amortization schedule, in which a rise in interest rate results in the additional

interest being added on to your principal. Such types of ARMs should be avoided.

❏ Find out whether the ARM can be converted to a fixed-rate loan, and at what price. Ideally, you should be able to convert the loan if desired without going through the entire loan-application process all over again.

❏ Make sure there is no prepayment penalty on the loan.

❏ Ideally, the loan will be assumable.

ALPHABET SOUP

In addition to fixed-rate mortgages and adjustable-rate mortgages, there are many other types of mortgage loans—GPMs, GPAMs, FLEXs, DILs, SAMs, PLAMs, RRMs, FLIPs, GEMs, and on and on. Most of these are variations on one theme or another. Here are brief descriptions of several such alternative mortgages:

Renegotiable Rate Mortgages (RRMs), also known as **rollover mortgages**, are a kind of adjustable-rate mortgage—actually, a series of ARMs. With an RRM, you get a series of short-term loans, which are renegotiable every three to five years. The interest rate may change with each negotiation, although there are caps of a half percentage point for each year of the renegotiation period, and a lifetime cap of 5 percent increase. As with ARMs, these loans start out lower than conventional mortgages, but run the risk of running considerably higher if rates skyrocket.

Graduated Payment Mortgages (GPMs) are fixed-rate mortgages that feature lower monthly payments in the early years and somewhat higher payments in the later years. Payments rise gradually over the course of the loan until they reach a fixed level. These loans are specifically designed for young, first-time buyers who may be hard-pressed to make payments in early years, but whose rising incomes down the road should be sufficient to cover payments. For example, the monthly payments may be reduced 17 percent for the first two years, 10 percent in years three and four, 5 percent in year five, and then *rise* 3 percent for the remaining life of the loan; the exact percentages vary from lender to lender. The bottom line is that the total amount spent will be more than with a conventional mortgage, both in the higher monthly payment in later years and in the total money paid. GPMs often come with restrictions; the loan may be for a first-time buyer or the home may need to be owner-occupied. There is usually a minimum 10 percent down payment requirement. The FHA has a limited program for insuring GPMs.

Graduated Payment Adjustable Mortgages (GPAMs) represent a combination of GPMs and ARMs. That is, they feature lower monthly payments in early years, like GPMs, but the interest rates are adjusted periodically, as with ARMs. These are somewhat riskier, particularly for young buyers, if interest rates shoot up. With rates kept low during early years regardless of interest rate rises, it could result in negative amortization if there are significant rate increases during the first few years.

Shared Appreciation Mortgages (SAMs) in effect let the lender own part of your house. In exchange for a below-market interest rate, you agree to share the appreciation of your house— the amount it increases in value between the time you buy it and sell it or the loan reaches maturity. In a typical arrangement, the lender might give you a loan 30 percent below prevailing rates— 7 percent, for example, when most people are paying 10 percent. For this privilege, you agree to give the lender 30 percent of the profits when you sell the house, or after a stated period—say, eight years. If you haven't moved as of that time, the lender would refinance the house—based on an appraiser's determination of the house's market value—to cover the unpaid balance of the mortgage plus the lump sum you'd have to pay the lender under the arrangement.

These loans are controversial for both parties. On the lender's side, it involves lending money at a rate that may be below what the lender has paid for it—for example, it may have borrowed that 7 percent mortgage money at 7.5 percent. And there is considerable risk for borrowers: Aside from having to fork over a good chunk of the profits on your house, you may end up with a high-interest-rate loan at the time of refinancing. And if the property does not appreciate, you still may be liable for paying the lender a fee for the low interest rate you were given originally.

Price-Level Adjusted Mortgages (PLAMs) may seem like a good idea, but they're usually far from it. These loans are fixed at an extremely low interest rate, but the loan principal—and, thus, your monthly payments—are adjusted for inflation. The increase is added to the principal, not the interest rate. The idea is to make your monthly payments in "real" dollars—dollars that aren't worth less each year as inflation creeps up. So, if the annual inflation rate were 4 percent, your monthly payments would rise accordingly. Of course, if inflation heats up—and there are plenty of people who believe that is always possible, due to a host of national and international circumstances—your monthly payments could get well out of hand. Another disadvantage of PLAMs is that when rates rise, you don't get the benefit of deducting additional interest on your taxes, as you would with an ARM, in which you pay higher interest when rates go up.

Reverse Annuity Mortgages (RAMs) are designed for older homeowners who have been paying off their mortgages for years. They are designed as a means of putting the equity you build up to work in your later years, when your income may be substantially decreased. In this kind of mortgage, the lender actually pays *you*. Each month for a period of five to fifteen years, you are paid a predetermined sum—perhaps $1,000 or more. At the same time, you continue to make mortgage payments, but for a much smaller amount. At the end of the predetermined period (or upon the death of the owner), when the loan becomes due, you can either refinance the house or sell it and pay back the lender. So, with a RAM, you're effectively being paid the appreciation and equity on your house while you still live there.

Flexible Loan Insurance Programs (FLIPs) are somewhat like Graduated Payment Mortgages, with the added feature that you put part of your down payment into a savings account. Each month, the lender will withdraw a few dollars of that down payment to supplement the low interest rate of your monthly payments; the payments rise gradually over the first few years, becoming somewhat higher than a conventional mortgage after about five years. But because the savings feature helps reduce mortgage payments by as much as a fourth in the first few years, it allows a lot of people who wouldn't otherwise qualify to be able to afford a loan.

Flexible Payment Mortgages (FLEXs) involve interest-only payments during the first five years. In subsequent years, monthly payments are increased to make up for lost principal payments. As with Graduated Payment Mortgages (see below), these are intended for buyers who expect to have higher income in future years. And because the first few years' worth of mortgage payments contain only a very small percentage of principal payments anyway, there isn't as much unpaid principal to make up for as you'd imagine.

Deferred Interest Loans (DILs) are the reverse of FLEX loans. With a DIL, you pay a low interest rate in the first few years, and higher in later years, but the additional interest is tacked on to the total mortgage. As with GPMs, they assume that you'll have a higher income in a few years.

Shared Equity Loan Programs (SHAREs) create a partnership or joint venture between you and the lender. In a SHARE mortgage, you purchase 80 percent of the house outright and lease the remaining 20 percent from the lender or developer. The holder of the 20 percent share collects a nominal rent each month, but the payments remain less than what a full mortgage would cost. And you have an option to buy that 20 percent share at some future date, although the price will reflect any appreciation in the house's value. Because you are buying only 80 percent of the property, the lower monthly payments—and the lower qualifying income—may easily constitute the difference between being able to afford and not being able to afford buying the property. On a $75,000 house, for example, the annual income you'd need to qualify for a mortgage would be about $5,000 less with a SHARE mortgage than with a conventional thirty-year mortgage.

Growing Equity Mortgages (GEMs) combine a fixed interest rate with a changing monthly payment. The increased monthly payment is based on an agreed-upon schedule or a common index, such as the Commerce Department's index that measures after-tax, per capita income. But the extra money you pay over and above the base amount goes directly toward paying off the principal. For example, if your mortgage payments are $600 a month, and you agree to a 5 percent annual rise, your monthly payment the second year will rise to $630. But that extra $30 a month will go directly toward the loan's balance, not as interest, so you'll end up paying the mortgage off well before the thirty-year maturity date.

Balloon Mortgages involve a small monthly payment, followed by a large lump-sum payment on some fixed date. Seven- and ten-year balloons have low payments, because they are calculated as if the loan will be paid off in thirty years. (Some balloon loans may be as short as three years.) In some balloon mortgages, the payments are interest-only. However, at the end of the seven- or ten-year period, the unpaid balance comes due; usually it requires refinancing or selling the property. These mortgages can be ideal if you don't plan to stay in the house for more than a few years, and if you are sure that you will be able to handle the balloon when it comes due.

Easy Qualifying (EQUAL) Mortgages are variations on the GPM: They are fixed-rate mortgages with lower payments built into the early years. The lower payments are made up for through agreed-upon increments in later years, usually increasing at a gradual rate. But one big difference from GPMs is that under no circumstances can EQUAL mortgages accumulate negative amortization. The reason is something called the "buy-down" account. To do this, you must set aside between 3 and 6 percent of the house's purchase price into a separate interest-earning account. The interest earned subsidizes the loan, thereby lowering monthly payments to permit lower interest rates in the early years. In many cases, the buy-down amount is contributed by the builder or developer (for a newly built home) or the realty agent or seller. The exact terms of the EQUAL loan are custom-tailored to your specific needs, thanks to a computer program that plugs in a variety of possible payment schedules and alternative interest rates. The down side of EQUAL mortgages is that the monthly payment rises to slightly above what it would be under a conventional mortgage around the fifth year. But EQUALs aren't designed for savings; they're intended to qualify those who otherwise might not qualify for a mortgage.

As stated earlier, the number of types of mortgages continues to grow. You should check with lenders, realty agents, and others to find the newest and most innovative plans that may be suited to your particular needs. It's important with any of these mortgages that you ask the lender to compare their terms and costs to a conventional mortgage. The fact is, good old fashioned thirty-year conventional mortgages are still the loans of choice for most home buyers.

ACCELERATED PAYMENT PLANS

The above statement notwithstanding, there are an increasing number of variations on conventional mortgages. Here are two:

❏ *Shorter time periods.* Ten-, fifteen-, and twenty-year mortgages are now becoming increasingly common, intended for borrowers who want to pay off their loans quickly at a lower interest rate, and pay less interest over the life of the loan. (Remember that the shorter the period for which lenders must commit themselves to an interest rate, the lower the rate will be.) But these shorter, fixed-rate mortgages aren't for everyone. They are best suited for buyers for whom monthly payments won't be a problem, and who don't intend to remain in their homes for more than a dozen years. Another consideration is your tax bracket: Shorter loans work best for those in lower tax brackets, because there's less advantage in the higher interest write-offs of a longer-period loan. (Of course, you've probably noted the paradox: Those in lower tax brackets usually aren't those for whom monthly payments won't be a problem.) Because these loans lock you into a higher monthly payment schedule than with a thirty-year loan, such mortgages must be considered carefully.

❑ *Less time between payments.* Who says you need to pay your mortgage only once a month? In a biweekly mortgage, you make half of your regular monthly payments every two weeks. Because that amounts to twenty-six payments—or thirteen months—a year, you'd pay off the mortgage in just under twenty-one years, at a considerable savings in interest. For example, a thirty-year $80,000 mortgage at 10 percent interest would result in $172,000 in interest over the life of the loan. Paid biweekly, the loan would be paid off in twenty years and nine months, with only $110,000 in interest—a savings of over $60,000. But, as with the shorter mortgages described above, biweekly mortgages lock you into increased spending that could cause problems someday if your income were to be decreased or temporarily cut off. But if you are paid every two weeks by your employer, the schedule of payments—which are usually electronically deducted from your checking account—may be ideal.

Experts warn that you should think twice—or thrice—before embarking on any of these plans. Because the interest rate on mortgages will almost always be cheaper than that for any other kind of loan you can get, you might be better off taking the extra money you'd otherwise pay to accelerate your mortgage and invest it elsewhere. And if inflation or interest rates take off, your fixed-rate mortgage will be more valuable than ever, because you'll be paying off borrowed money at below-market rates or with inflated (less valuable) dollars. If interest rates plunge by more than a couple points, you may best be served by refinancing your present mortgage.

Again, your financial planner, tax consultant, lender, or attorney may offer sage advice on these matters, and you are strongly urged to consult one of these professionals before deciding the kind of mortgage that is best for you.

HELP FROM FAMILY AND FRIENDS

These days, it is becoming increasingly rare that first-time home buyers can afford the initial costs of home ownership without help. The down payment, closing costs, and moving costs have placed home ownership beyond the reach of a growing number of people. It's not uncommon for strapped home seekers to turn to family and friends for help. This is nothing new. For generations, parents and grandparents—as well as aunts, uncles, cousins, and siblings—have helped their children and grandchildren to afford their first home, whether in the form of an outright gift of money to apply to the initial purchase price, through a low-interest loan, through an equity-sharing arrangement, or some other creative alternative.

We're treading on personal ground here, to be sure. Not all relatives should enter into such arrangements, considering the emotional baggage that sometimes accompanies family money matters. There are endless issues involved, from personal philosophies to issues of psychological freedom and pride. On the other hand, don't be bashful. Your family may be delighted to help, if only you'd ask. If your benefactors are friends, you've got other things to think about before you enter into business arrangements. In any case, you'll need to create some paperwork, even if the money is a gift, to appease your lender and the IRS. Here are some typical arrangements:

❑ *Borrowing*. If you borrow money from family or friends, sign a note—you can write your own or obtain a preprinted one for a few cents at many stationery stores—just as if you were borrowing money from a bank. Most likely, the loan will be for a relatively short period, say, two to five years, although it can be for as long as you'd like. The loan may involve regular monthly payments, interest-only payments with a balloon payment upon maturity, or a full balloon payment, with principal and interest due upon maturity.

❑ *Gifts*. Federal tax laws allow you to receive up to $10,000 a year in gift money from someone without declaring it as income. In some families, such gifts are appropriate ways to pass along a family estate prior to parents' death. If the amount involved is greater than $10,000, you may be able to comply with federal laws by receiving the maximum in one year, and borrowing the balance as a loan, which may be forgiven in subsequent years, so that no more than $10,000 is given in any year. (However, there are ways to get more than ten grand in gift money tax-free. The law sets the $10,000 limit on a per-person basis. So, two parents can each give the same child $10,000 *per person*, or $20,000 total;

in fact, each of two parents can give each partner of a married couple $10,000 each—for a total of $40,000 in tax-free gift-money—as well as giving the maximum amount to each child in the same family. So if resources permit, the limit can be extended creatively—and perfectly legally.) If money is being given as a gift, you'll need to obtain a letter stating that the money needn't be repaid, so the lender knows that you aren't being burdened with additional monthly loan payments that might affect your ability to repay your mortgage.

❑ *Co-signing.* A third option is for your family or friends to co-sign your mortgage. By doing so, they will be legally responsible for making payments in the event you default on your mortgage. But choosing the right co-signer is important, too: That individual must have significant income to meet the demands of the mortgage, in the lender's eyes. And simply being well-off may not qualify one to be a co-signer. Some lenders, for example, won't allow retired parents to co-sign children's loans, no matter how wealthy those parents might be. If the parents have no substantial *income* to cover the mortgage, they may not qualify.

❑ *Collateral.* Another way friends or family may help is to put up assets as collateral against a second mortgage. If, for example, your parents' house is nearly paid off, and they have no intention of selling it for some years, they may be willing to use it to guarantee a second mortgage—one to cover your down payment and closing costs, for example. That second mortgage will likely be for a relatively short period—say, under ten years. After a few years, when your income may have increased and you've paid down the mortgage and established your credit worthiness, the lender may be willing to remove the collateral from the loan. It's important to understand that as long as the property is used as collateral, it may not be sold. Real estate, however, isn't the only thing that may be used as collateral. Stocks, bonds, and certain other investments usually may be offered as well.

USING YOUR OWN EQUITY
Don't forget about assets you may already have that might be used as collateral for a second mortgage. Stocks, bonds, life

insurance policies, jewelry, Treasury bills, certificates of deposit, even your car may be sufficient to obtain the few thousand dollars you need for the down payment or closing costs.

LETTING THE SELLER HELP

Still another important source of money to help you afford a house is the seller of the property you're buying. In many cases, the seller may be willing to participate in the financing, either to increase the marketability of the property, or to gain some additional income out of the sale. Among the possibilities:

❏ *Loan assumption.* One of the easiest solutions is to assume the seller's loan. Most loans made before 1980 and some loans made since then are "assumable"—their terms may be taken over by someone other than the loan applicant, including the buyer of the property. And many of those assumable loans are extremely attractive—5 or 6 percent, for example. On the other hand, if the seller has owned the house a while, he or she has built up considerable equity, which you'll have to pay in the form of a substantial down payment. For example, you may be buying an $80,000 home, for which the owner has a $35,000 mortgage balance at 6 percent interest. To assume the loan, you'll have to come up with $45,000 in cash to pay the seller. It may be possible to take out a second mortgage for that amount at current interest rates. The difference in monthly payments of the two loans—the 6 percent loan and the current-market-rate one—should be significantly below what you'd pay if you got a mortgage for the full amount at current rates. Of course, the seller, realizing that the assumable mortgage is worth something to you, will likely want to be compensated for the low-interest gift—probably in the form of a higher selling price. You should be aware that laws governing assumable loans vary from state to state.

❏ *Second mortgage.* Second mortgages are available from a variety of sources, and the seller is as good a source as any. The second mortgage, which most likely will be used to supplement the down payment when obtaining your principal mortgage, can be arranged in a variety of ways. Most advantageous to you, particularly during the first few years of owning a home, is for the loan to be spread out over, say, five years, paying interest only every month, with a balloon payment due after five years (although it could be repayable as little as one year after, or as long as ten). Presumably, after that time, you'll be on more stable financial ground, or your house will have appreciated sufficiently so that you could refinance it and pay off the second mortgage. There are variations even on this theme, such as amortizing the five-year loan over a thirty-year period, meaning your monthly payments would be the same size as if you had a thirty-year loan; then, in effect, you prepay the loan after five years. The possibilities are many and varied. Keep in mind that your primary lender will likely place limits on the amount you can borrow as a second mortgage, probably no more than 10 percent of the purchase price, assuming you are making a 20 percent down payment. The lender's obvious concern is that you'll be able to make payments on both loans.

❑ *Wraparound mortgage.* When the seller's mortgage isn't assumable, one good arrangement is the wraparound. Let's say you are paying $100,000 on a house, for which the seller has a $35,000 mortgage. The seller would take back all the financing but would keep paying off the original mortgage, presumably one with an attractive low-interest rate. And let's say you put down 20 percent and assume monthly payments of about $800 a month for the $80,000 mortgage. The seller takes that $800 and makes monthly payments of $300 on the original mortgage and keeps the remaining $500. In effect, you have "wrapped" your mortgage around the seller's. But keep in mind that the seller's lender may not approve of this arrangement; if the original mortgage has a "due on sale" clause, the seller would be required to pay off the original mortgage when title of the house is transferred to you.

❑ *Rent with the option to buy.* This is a novel arrangement that can work well for both parties. In a rent-with-option arrangement, you rent the property with the right to purchase it at a specific price within a specific time period. In the ideal arrangement, all or part of your rent would be applied to the down payment. This situation works best during a time of high interest rates, allowing you to buy time until rates come back down to a reasonable level, or when the seller wants to temporarily forego income to delay or avoid capital gains taxes. There's some risk, of course, that time will run out on your rental period and you still won't have adequate or reasonable financing. The rent-with-option route can be particularly attractive if you are moving to a new city and don't have a lot of time to explore new neighborhoods. By renting first, you can "try out" a neighborhood—as well as a house—before deciding whether it's right for you.

All seller-financing plans require some careful thought, as well as good legal and financial advice. Carefully and thoughtfully executed, seller financing can provide the best possible arrangement for both buyer and seller.

OTHER FINANCING POSSIBILITIES

The list goes on. Each of these gets a bit trickier or riskier than those mentioned above, and you are urged to examine each one carefully before proceeding.

❑ *Get an investor*. This can be anyone from a relative to a relative stranger, although the potential legal land mines in such arrangements warrant that you shouldn't pick just anyone. An investor would put up a percentage of the money and receive a percentage of the ownership and tax benefits; you, presumably, would make all the mortgage payments, although the investor would likely co-sign the loan. So, you'd get your house (or at least a portion of it) with little or no down payment and without much of a financing problem. When you sell the house, profits are divvied up according to ownership percentages. You might even include in your contract with the investor the ability to buy him or her out at a specific price within a given time period. You'll need a lawyer to draw up papers that will reduce the likelihood of problems down the road.

❑ *Get a fixer-upper*. This, of course, is almost redundant: Most homes require you to put some work into them before they are truly satisfactory. But some homes require a *lot* of work, and these are often referred to in ads as "fixer-uppers" or the ever-popular "handyman's special." In some such cases, you are buying little more than a glorified shell, requiring you to put in more money than you paid for it in the first place. But the total price may be less than you would have paid for a comparable home, and you'll have the added satisfaction of having fixed it up to your tastes. The bad news, other than the fact that you may have to live in semisqualor during the renovation, is that you aren't likely to get a mortgage for this purchase without adequate blueprints, qualified contractors, and proof that you'll be able to pay for both the mortgage and the construction loan.

❏ *Build your own.* This may not be as outrageous as it sounds. Buying a lot and contracting out the construction could cost less than a comparable new home, particularly if you purchase land in a less-populated area. But building your own home presents a host of potential problems that can't adequately be addressed here, not the least of which is financing.

❏ *Buy something with rental income.* It defies logic, but if you can't afford a house yourself, it might make more sense to buy *two* and rent one out. More than likely, this will be in the form of a duplex—two connected houses—or a house with attached or adjacent rental property. The profit from the rental income could subsidize your own housing costs. Again, this will require some financing hocus-pocus.

❏ *Shop the foreclosure market.* This isn't for the fainthearted, but there are some real bargains to be had. Foreclosed properties—also known as REOs, for "real estate owned"—are those taken back by lenders through foreclosures against defaulting mortgage borrowers. Such homes are offered for sale at cut-rate prices by the federal government—notably, the Federal Housing Administration and the Veterans Administration—and by several private companies that buy these orphaned residences from lenders. They can be found at all price ranges and in all parts of the country, with concentrations in boom-or-bust states such as Texas, California, Florida, Oklahoma, and Arizona. In some cases, the sellers of these properties can arrange financing, often at very reasonable terms. But shopping the foreclosure market means being able to carefully inspect a property in a hurry, and to assess its value accurately. Obviously, you'll be somewhat limited as to specific locations, so you won't likely find such a property in the neighborhood of your dreams.

A FINAL THOUGHT

As you can see, the financial aspects of home buying could fill a book in itself; indeed, there are several books on just this subject. And with good reason: When you are buying something as expensive and as legally complex as a house, there ought to be a number of alternatives. The key is to look at all the possibilities and find the one that's best for you. Despite all the "new," "alternative," and "creative" mortgages, you may find when all is said and done that the old reliable thirty-year, fixed-rate, conventional mortgage is the one for you. And that's a perfectly wonderful realization.

Whatever the financial route to your purchase, the prospect of committing yourself to a thirty-year (or whatever) loan can be nerve-racking, particularly for first-timers. And the increased monthly payment—from the rental or less expensive home in which you are now residing to this relatively expensive new purchase—can seem overwhelming at first. The good news is that you'll get used to it: What may seem like a huge monthly payment right now will seem reasonable in a few years, and a bargain a few years farther down the road.

Chapter 7
Signing, Sealing, Delivering

Before you sign the final papers and take possession of your new home, there's one final procedure: inspection.

Why, you might be asking, should you wait until now—after you've signed a purchase agreement and secured financing—to thoroughly inspect the property? In the early stages of your house search, your inspections, however thorough, probably were somewhat superficial. Unless you hired a professional inspector, you likely did not climb through the attic, check the foundation, or spot-check the electrical system for potential problems. These are types of things that the home inspector will turn up, things a fresh coat of paint cannot hide.

In your purchase agreement, you should have included a clause stating that the sale of the house is contingent upon an inspection—actually, several inspections. One or more of these inspections, in fact, may be required by your lender before they will sign off on the mortgage. Now is the moment of truth: someone will pass judgment on what this house is all about.

But who will that someone be? There are home inspectors and home inspectors, with different credentials and levels of experience. Given that the price of a typical inspection—usually under $250—is trivial when considering a $50,000 or $100,000 purchase, you are urged *not* to cut corners in this area. If you really want to know, only the best qualified inspector should be hired. In fact, you should shop for an inspector as carefully as you shop for a home.

As always, ask around. Real estate agents, lenders, lawyers, and friends often have recommendations. (But be careful: An inspector who gets referrals from the selling agent may not want to "find" anything to ruin the agent's sale.) Or check the Yellow Pages under "Building Inspectors" or "Building Inspection Services." When calling, ask for credentials and references. The inspector should employ licensed engineers and architects.

Favor those inspectors who belong to the American Society of Home Inspectors (ASHI), which establishes standards of practice and requires that its members subscribe to a code of ethics. (For a list of its members, write to ASHI, 1010 Wisconsin Avenue NW, Washington, DC 20007.)

The inspection should take a couple hours or so. It's a good idea to be present at the inspection, although this generally isn't required. By following the inspector around the house, by observing and asking questions, you will learn about your new home, perhaps even get a few candid comments that wouldn't otherwise show up in the inspection report. The inspector may offer suggested solutions to problems, perhaps even recommending reliable contractors.

The inspector's written report will make for interesting reading, even if everything is ship-shape. It will describe the home's basic components and systems—roof, foundation, attic, basement, electrical, plumbing, heating, cooling, insulation, kitchen appliances, and all the rest—describing them in some technical detail. Included with that description should be the approximate date of installation or construction and the estimated remaining life for each item. For example, it might state that "The existing 150-amp electrical service with circuit breakers should be sufficient for most present and reasonably anticipated future needs." Or that the house "has a galvanized steel gutter and downspout system which is in poor condition; the system should be replaced." The inspector should also include cost estimates for fixing the flaws, which will come in handy during the final negotiations. Some inspectors even estimate replacement and repair costs for up to five years.

Don't panic if there are a few relatively minor defects; nearly all homes have them. Of course, it is always your option to back out of the deal at this point and get your down payment back—that is what the inspection contingency in the purchase agreement was all about. More than likely, however, you'll want to take some less-drastic action. You have two basic choices to make:

❑ *Get things fixed.* You may ask the seller to make the necessary repairs or replacements prior to settlement. If so, make sure that the agreement specifies the quality and nature of the work to be done, so that the job meets professional standards.

❏ *Lower the price.* After determining the costs to fix or replace flawed items, you can negotiate with the seller. Ideally, you will be able to deduct these reasonable costs from the selling price. (Or, you may be given a credit toward the down payment.) After settlement, you can make the repairs yourself.

FINAL INSPECTIONS
In addition to the overall inspection, there are other, more specific inspections that should be done prior to closing, some of which may be required by the lender or state or local housing laws. Ideally, you should have specified these inspections as a contingency in the purchase agreement. They include:

❏ *Termites.* In most parts of the country, termite inspection is required prior to settlement. The seller usually will pay the $500 or so cost of the inspection, and will be expected to remedy all infestation problems before the sale is completed.

❏ *Radon.* This is a more recent concern, and few housing laws address it. Radon is a radioactive, cancer-causing gas that is a natural component of rock, soil, and some building materials. In some parts of the country, radon is being found to build up in sufficient concentrations to create potentially serious health problems, particularly in energy-efficient houses, in which insulation and caulking make it difficult for the radon to vent into the atmosphere. There are several do-it-yourself radon inspection kits on the market for under $35; usually, they require your leaving the testing device in your basement for a few days, then sending the canister off to a testing lab, which then sends you a report with the results. But this can take a few weeks to complete. Faster—and more accurate—is a professionally done inspection, although this will cost $100 or more. (Look for labs accredited by the National Institute for Occupational Safety and Health, an agency of the federal government.) There's a good chance that either type of test will find some radon in the house, although it's the concentration that's important; a low concentration probably won't be a problem, particularly if it's limited to the basement. If it's a moderate or high level, some remedy will be needed; depending on the exact level and the nature of the house, the remedy can cost anywhere from one hundred dollars to tens of thousands. Again, a professional radon inspector will be able to best interpret the results and suggest remedies.

WARRANTIES

Home warranties are a relatively new phenomenon, particularly for existing (as opposed to newly built) homes. But they are available and they may make sense for you, especially if they provide you with peace of mind.

Warranties—whether for a house, a car, or a TV—are a kind of insurance policy. Sometimes, the "policy" is built into the product, such as with a TV, which includes a warranty with the purchase price. (There often are extended warranties available from the retailer, which may or may not be worth the price.) To be worth more than the paper on which it's written, any warranty should cover

❑ one or more specific parts of the house
❑ for a specific period of time
❑ under specific conditions.

"Specific," as you can see, is a key word here. Many warranties aren't specific at all, and these are the ones that can get you into the most trouble. Some include vague terms that sound like one thing but mean something else completely when it comes time to make a warranty claim. Most real estate agents can arrange a one-year home warranty through any of several reputable third-party insurance companies. But keep in mind that even the best of these policies won't cover 100 percent of the things that can go wrong during your first year of ownership. More than likely, they'll cover most major systems: the wiring, plumbing, heating, and major appliances; air conditioning may cost extra. But they may *not* cover such essential parts of the house as the roof, the foundation, the structure, and the portions of the plumbing system located outside the house itself.

If the house has been adequately inspected by a professional, such policies may not be worth the $250-to-$500 cost. However, you may insist that the seller or the real estate agent pay for such a warranty as a condition of sale. Sellers and agents increasingly are likely to agree to this if it improves the chances of a sale.

MOVING IN BEFORE SETTLEMENT

Sometimes, circumstances make it necessary to move into your new home before settlement. This is often the case if you've just sold your existing home (or given notice to your landlord on a rental) and there has been some delay in settling on your new one. Minor delays are a fact of life with real estate. Given the various players involved—buyer, seller, agent, lawyer, lender, accountant, inspectors, appraiser, perhaps a building contractor—it isn't surprising that deadlines can slip by a few days or even weeks.

If you are buying a brand new home, you must be careful. Builders have been notorious for moving people into still-unfinished homes with vague agreements to finish "soon." But you have a lot less clout with the builder to finish things on time—and to your satisfaction—once you've moved in. And your own definition of "finished" and "on time" may be a lot different from the builder's. If you must move in, sign an agreement that's been reviewed first by your lawyer; the agreement should specify the settlement date. The builder will require you to pay rent during this period; that rent should stop on the day settlement is to take place.

If you're moving into an existing home, you still must protect yourself, particularly if you are relying on the seller to do inspections or make repairs or renovations. Again, a good lawyer-approved agreement is essential.

GOING TO SETTLEMENT

This is the day it all happens: You pay your money, sign the papers, and the house becomes legally yours. However simple that may sound, settlement (also known as closing) can be a complicated, time-consuming process, and it should be approached as seriously as any other aspect of buying a home.

Settlement practices vary from locality to locality, and even within the same county or city. Depending on location, settlements may be conducted by lending institutions, title-insurance companies, escrow companies, real estate brokers, and attorneys for either the buyer or seller. Needless to say, whoever conducts settlement will be paid handsomely for the effort, although the amount will vary widely, and you can save hundreds of dollars by shopping around. Between the time you apply for a mortgage and go to settlement, there usually is plenty of time to do such shopping.

Depending upon the state or city in which it takes place, settlement may seem like the final scene in a mystery movie, in which everyone you've seen throughout the film shows up at the same time in one room. There may be you, the buyer (and if there are more than one of you buying—even a husband and wife—both parties should attend); the seller; lawyers for both parties; the real estate agent; a representative of the lender; a representative of the title insurance company; and probably a notary public for good luck. Depending on local law, however, it may not be necessary for all parties to meet at the same time.

To make sure that everything goes according to plan at settlement, there are a few things you should check a few days before the big day:

❑ Are all inspections done?
❑ Have you inspected the house one last time a day or two before closing to make sure everything is in order?
❑ Has the title search been completed?
❑ Have you secured all necessary insurance?
❑ Have you secured your financing?
❑ Will your lawyer be available to accompany you?
❑ Do *you* know where and when to show up?
❑ Will the seller have moved out by that date?

CLOSING COSTS

At settlement, besides swapping money for title, there is a rather lengthy list of fees that must be paid. Known in their entirety as closing costs, they add up to the third-largest cost of home buying—perhaps $5,000 or more, money you won't be able to finance as part of your mortgage. Who pays for them—buyer or seller—is largely a matter of negotiation, although the bulk of them usually become the burden of the buyer; some of this is determined by local custom.

When you apply for a mortgage, the lender is required by federal law to provide you with a good-faith estimate of settlement service charges you will likely incur, as well as the name, address, and phone number of each provider of services that the lender will employ in the process. You will also receive a free copy of the U.S. Department of Housing and Urban Development's *HUD Guide to Home Buyers*. The estimate provided by the lender may be stated as either a dollar amount or as a range for each charge. If the costs are stated as a range, you should ask the lender where in the range your actual costs will fall. But even this estimate may not cover all the items you will end up paying at settlement.

One day before settlement, you have the right to examine a standard government-provided form, the Disclosure/Settlement Statement, also known as HUD-1, detailing the actual closing costs; however, some exact costs won't yet be known, and they may not be included.

Here is a breakdown of key closing costs. Keep in mind that you are free to do your own comparison shopping.

❏ *Title search fee.* The title search is an official history of the ownership of the property you are buying to ensure there isn't any legal question that the home belongs to the seller; you don't want to wake up one morning to hear that someone else is claiming ownership of "your" house. The search usually is conducted by a title-insurance company or a lawyer, the latter's services usually being the more expensive. You may be well served by calling two or more title insurance companies (listed in the Yellow Pages) or lawyers to find out their standard fees for this service.

❏ *Title insurance.* Unfortunately, the title search is not 100 percent proof that the title is free and clear. There are certain "defects" in title that may not show up in a search, ranging from forged documents to a host of technical factors that aren't worth going into here. So, while the chances of defective title may be next to nil, title insurance is in order to protect you against even that remote possibility. There are two kinds of policies: lender's insurance, which likely will be required to protect your lender, and owner's insurance, which is optional. Local custom dictates whether the buyer or seller pays for this. Whoever pays can save money by shopping around, although the cheapest policy may be found from the insurance company that did the title search. There is a one-time premium, which protects you and your heirs as long as you retain any interest in the property. Ask about a reissue rate, a special discounted rate that may be available if the property changed hands recently; you'll probably need the policy number of the previous owner to qualify for the discount.

❑ *Property survey*. A survey is a kind of map, detailing the exact dimensions and location of the lot on which the house sits. Your lenders may require a survey; you also will probably need one at settlement. While the cost is minimal—usually under $100— you may save money by locating the surveyor who previously surveyed the property. It may be possible to simply update the old survey, rather than drawing a completely new one.

❑*Attorney's fees*. Regardless of whether or not you hire a lawyer, you'll have to pay the lender's and title company's legal fees—the cost of preparing and recording legal documents. Sometimes these fees amount to little more than the use of an attorney's office, where settlement might take place. Still, there is no way around paying this.

❑ *Bank charges*. We've already covered points, also known as loan origination fees. They are fees paid to lenders to cover administrative costs and bolster profit. The number of points you'll have to pay on your loan will range from one to as many as four; the seller also may be charged one point. Other bank fees include a credit report fee (the cost of obtaining your credit record) and an appraisal fee (the cost of the lender's independent appraisal).

❑ *Assumption fee*. If you're assuming someone else's mortgage, you'll have to pay a fee of a few hundred dollars, which covers processing costs. The fee is often one percent of the loan.

❑ *Inspection fees.* You may already have paid some of these, or they may be taken care of at settlement. These, as stated earlier, are negotiable: you may get the seller to pay some or all of these fees.

❑ *Recording and transfer charges.* These are state and local fees and vary from area to area. Basically, such charges cover the cost of recording the deed in your name, among other administrative tasks. When it comes down to it, however, they are simply a tax on home buying—a means of generating income for state and local governments.

❑ *Homeowner's insurance.* Most lenders require that you purchase insurance against fire, flood, hurricanes, theft, and other calamities. The lender—or your real estate agent or lawyer—may even offer a policy that covers these basic needs. If so, you should shop around before signing on; such policies usually include a hefty profit for the sponsoring individual or company. You may do much better by going direct to any major insurance company or independent agent and get the best coverage at the best price. When shopping, it is important to understand the many exclusions contained in homeowner's coverage. Ask the agent to provide material—and "translations," if necessary, into plain English—explaining the terms of the policy. Among other things, you'll want to make sure that the policy has an automatic escalator clause, increasing the amount of coverage as your property increases in value.

❑ *Prepaid items.* This includes a potpourri of things that must be paid in advance. They may include:

> ✔ special assessments for street or sewer improvements
> ✔ interest from the date of closing to the beginning of the period covered by the first mortgage payment
> ✔ the first premium on private mortgage insurance
> ✔ the first premium on homeowner's insurance
> ✔ the first six months' property taxes

❏ *Other fees.* These can include everything from notary fees to escrow fees and life insurance—even the cost of a photographer taking a picture of the property.

Despite the concise, standardized summary sheet outlining closing costs, there's nothing simple about the paperwork for closings. Each of the above costs seems to involve another piece of paper for you to read and/or sign. It's an endless parade of paper, all of which should be read by you and your lawyer. Inevitably, there will be something missing, a state of affairs that may take anywhere from a few minutes to a few days to rectify.

Among the things you will be signing at closing is the mortgage note (the promise to repay the loan in regular monthly amounts on a timely basis) and the "deed of trust" (the legal document giving the lender the right to take back your property if you fail to make your mortgage payments). You will then be "loaned" the money to pay the seller for the property. The lender's agent will collect closing costs from you (with the blank check you brought with you) and give you a copy of the HUD-1 form. The deed will then be signed over to you and you will be given the keys to your new house. Don't rush out without making sure you've received a copy of *every* paper you've signed.

Congratulations! You have just purchased a house. Welcome home!

HOW TO SELL A HOUSE

HOW TO SELL A HOUSE

by
Joel Makower

A Tilden Press Book
published by
Perigee Books

Perigee Books
are published by
The Putnam Publishing Group
200 Madison Avenue
New York, NY 10016

Library of Congress Cataloging-in-Publication Data

Makower, Joel, date.
    How to buy a house / by Joel Makower. How to sell a house / by
Joel Makower.
       p.   cm.
    No collective t.p. Title transcribed from individual title pages.
    Two works bound together back-to-back.
    "A Tilden Press book."
    1. House buying.   2. House selling.   I. Makower, Joel, date.
How to sell a house.   1989.   II. Title.   III. Title: How to sell
a house.
    ISBN 0-399-51565-8
    HD1379.M353   1989   89-33668 CIP
    643' . 12—dc20

Printed in the United States of America

1   2   3   4   5   6   7   8   9   10

Contents

ACKNOWLEDGMENTS

Thanks to Linda Zaleskie, who provided valuable research and organization. Thanks especially to Frances Makower, agent extraordinaire, for her comments on the manuscript.

Preface

There comes a moment in practically every homeowner's life when it's time to sell. And when that moment arrives, it sets in motion a process that could be quick and profitable or one that can drag on and on with less than satisfactory results. This book is intended to maximize your profit and satisfaction.

In the pages that follow, we'll go through that process step by step. You'll learn the ins and outs of finding potential buyers and getting the best deal for your property. You'll learn the secrets of the experts and get some insight into some of the things to do—and not to do—when selling real estate.

This book will deal primarily with selling a house, although much of the information will apply equally to apartments, condominiums, and cooperatives. It assumes that you are selling a house that is your primary residence, not necessarily one that's purely an investment, although a great deal of information will be applicable to such sales as well. (Investment real estate, however, involves additional concerns that are beyond the scope of this book.)

As you'll learn, selling a house requires that you put together a team—most likely an agent, a lawyer, and an accountant, or reasonable substitutes who are able to fulfill those roles—whose purpose is to protect your interests and ensure that any deal meets your individual needs. Always keep in mind when reading this book and when consulting other sources of information on this subject that your best information will come from people working directly in your interest.

Also keep in mind that there are hundreds of laws dealing with real estate transactions—federal, state, and local. And these laws are subject to change on a regular basis. Of particular concern is the financial aspect of real estate: loan rates, loan types, and tax angles seem to change with the tides. It will be of vital importance that you or your advisers keep up to date on these matters.

Overall, the important thing to keep in mind when selling a house is that every home, and every individual, is unique. Your success as a seller will be directly related to your ability to keep your particular needs—and that of potential buyers—in mind at all times.

Chapter 1
Why Sell?

Do you really want to sell your house? That may seem like a simplistic question. "Of course I do," you may be saying. "That's why I'm reading this book."

Perhaps. But the question remains: Is selling your house really in your best interest? (If you are selling out of necessity—because you must move to another city, for example, or due to a major life change such as death or divorce—you may want to skip this section and move on to the next chapter.) The answer may not be as obvious as you think. There are several options you may want to consider before you go through the actual selling process. You may be surprised to find that some things you had considered impractical or unaffordable may in fact make perfect sense. Before you dive head first into the complexities of selling your house and finding another one, you may want to see if other options make better sense. It could save you a lot of time, trouble, and money in the process.

FIXING UP YOUR PRESENT HOME

For example, consider this: You may be better off fixing up, adding to, or otherwise altering your present house instead. According to a survey conducted by the National Association of Home Builders, the two main reasons homeowners seek another home are better energy efficiency and more space. Yet in many houses, both problems can be overcome.

There are countless ways to conserve energy: new windows and doors, weatherstripping and caulking, better insulation, new energy-efficient appliances, a new heating system, solar energy panels, and a host of other improvements. There are many books you can consult on the subject of saving energy and "retrofitting" your existing home in energy-saving ways. The money you'd invest in energy savings will likely pay for itself over time, or will improve the value of your house when you finally do decide to sell it. Moreover, if you need to borrow money

to make these improvements, you'll be able to deduct the interest you pay on the loan on your taxes.

Somewhat more ambitious, but even more rewarding, is to repair or remodel your present house to better suit your needs. After all, instead of searching and searching for a new house—which still probably won't exactly fit your ideal—why not take the place you now call home and *make* it fit your needs? You'll endure some discomfort, to be sure, but probably less than packing up, moving to a new house, and settling in a new neighborhood.

Start by making a wish list. Let your fantasies run wild: Another bedroom or two. An extra bathroom. The existing bathrooms remodeled. A new and bigger kitchen. A master bedroom suite. A new family room. A deck. A swimming pool. A hot tub. A new paint job inside and out. On the other hand, it may be that these things just aren't practical; your house has no room to grow, for example, or you'd rather simply start from scratch at a new location. And you may want to move to a specific new neighborhood or region.

But you might be surprised. By investing in your existing home, you'll do more than make it a more comfortable place to live. You'll also increase its value when you do decide to sell it. And you may be able to do all this for less than the cost of moving and buying a new place. It's probably worth spending some time talking to a contractor (most will give you a reasonable estimate at no charge) and to an accountant or other trusted financial counselor.

Your decision to remodel will have to do in part with how long you might remain in your present house. If you don't think you'll be living there for more than a year or two, you should limit your remodeling to "cosmetic" improvements—painting, wallpapering, and carpeting—that can be done relatively inexpensively; you might even do them yourself to keep costs to a minimum. For less than $5,000—maybe much less—you may be able to give your present home a fresh feeling that will postpone the need to find new quarters—perhaps until you are truly able to afford them.

How will you get the money to pay for more extensive remodeling? If you've owned your present home for more than a

few years, believe that the price of your present home has gone up, and know you've got reasonably good credit, you have at least two key choices: refinance your present home or borrow against its equity. Let's examine both.

❏ *Refinancing*. Simply put, refinancing means taking out a new mortgage—one big enough to pay off your existing mortgage as well as give you enough extra money to make the improvements you want to make. (You needn't use the money strictly for improvements, of course; you can do with the money whatever you'd like. We'll assume, however, that you don't want to borrow any more money than necessary.) So, let's say that you have $45,000 remaining on your original $65,000 mortgage, and that the appraised value of your house is now $95,000, about $15,000 more than you paid for it four years ago. By taking out a new mortgage for $76,000—80 percent of the property's appraised value—you could pay off the remaining $45,000 loan and have about $30,000 with which to fix your present abode.

Now for the bad news: You will now have a bigger mortgage, with bigger monthly payments. And the interest rate on your new mortgage will be at current market rates, which may be somewhat higher than your existing mortgage. Moreover, there will be closing costs associated with your new mortgage, including points—one point equals one percent of the mortgage—and possibly a prepayment penalty for paying off your existing mortgage early—that is, before its thirty-year maturity, or however long the term of your original mortgage.

Still, refinancing could make perfect sense, if you run the numbers. A lender—perhaps the same one that holds your current mortgage—probably will be delighted to give you the specific closing costs and monthly payment schedule. You might find that the bottom-line figure makes refinancing a much better deal. After all, if you were to move, you'd still have to pay the closing costs, the current interest rate, and a prepayment penalty. So you're no farther behind. What you won't have if you move is your present house.

One alternative to refinancing is getting a second mortgage. Most such mortgages are written for under $10,000, usually for a period of five to ten years. But interest rates for

second mortgages are somewhat higher than for first mortgages. Still, if you've built up equity, this may be a viable alternative.

❏ *Home equity loan.* This is similar to a second mortgage in that it lets you borrow against the equity you have in your present house. *Equity* refers to the current value of your house minus any outstanding debts. So, in the example offered above—in which there was a $45,000 mortgage remaining on a house appraised at $95,000—you would have $50,000 in equity, the amount you would keep if you were to sell the house, pay off the mortgage, and put the money in your pocket.

In the typical home equity loan, you can borrow up to 80 percent of the equity in your home—$40,000 in the above example. The loan would be secured by your house; if you were to default on the loan, the lender could sell your house and use the proceeds to pay off the original mortgage and the home equity loan (along with a host of legal costs). Again, there are some loan fees associated with these loans—points and closing costs, for example—and you must run the numbers to see if this can work for you. There are tax considerations on home equity loans, too, and you are advised to go over these with your accountant or tax preparer.

Home equity loans come in a wide variety. One is the reverse annuity mortgage or RAM, intended for homeowners who have paid off all or most of their mortgage. A sort of mortgage in reverse, a RAM pays *you* a monthly installment, part of which you then use to repay the loan. In the process, you have a monthly surplus, which you can use for whatever purpose you desire, from basic necessities to luxuries.

There are other sources for funds, including personal loans, which carry substantially higher interest rates than first or second mortgages or home equity loans. If they make sense, however, any such sources are worth considering.

In the end, you may decide that money isn't really the issue in deciding whether or not to find another house. For example, if you truly are ready to get your present house—or your present neighborhood—out of your life, there may be no dollar amount that could convince you to stay. On the other hand, if you're kind of sad to have to leave your house and neighbors, and would

prefer to find an alternative, refinancing or a home equity loan may be the way to go.

Renting It Out

Still another option to selling your home is to rent it out. That may seem impractical—after all, you'll need the money from your present house to buy another—but the fact is that you may be able to afford both.

Consider the refinancing option above. Suppose you were to take the $30,000 in excess money (the money remaining after you paid off your old mortgage with the proceeds from the new one) and used it as the down payment for your new house? Meanwhile, you'd rent out your present house—ideally, for enough money to cover the monthly payments. By holding on to your old place, you'd be able to retain its tax advantages (the interest deduction on the mortgage) as the house appreciated in value. There are a lot of experts who will flatly state that you can never own too much real estate.

The problem, of course, is whether the $30,000 (along with whatever other money you can scrape up) will cover the down payment and closing costs for your new house. (Your $30,000 would likely cover a 20 percent down payment on a $100,000 house, plus closing costs.) It may be that the numbers simply won't work. But then again, they might.

Renting out your house, by the way, is one very effective way of selling it, if the renter has an option to buy. In many such arrangements, a portion of each month's rent is credited toward a down payment, in effect allowing a would-be buyer to finance the down payment over time. (More on such arrangements in Chapter 5.) For many home buyers, renting with an option can put an otherwise unaffordable property within reach.

In the end, you may decide that selling your house is indeed the way to go. If so, fine. The considerations and calculations you've gone through were not for naught. You can now proceed to the next step with full knowledge that you are doing the right thing.

Chapter 2
With or Without an Agent?

Consider the home-selling process to be something of a well-orchestrated battle plan. Your chances of victory are directly linked to how well you prepare and execute that plan. You needn't make this a formal battle plan with forms, charts, maps, and diagrams; indeed, much of it needn't even be written down. But the more you prepare, the better off you'll be.

More than likely, one of your first key decisions in creating your battle plan is who, if anyone, you will hire to help you find a buyer. Put another way, will you enlist the services of a real estate agent or sell your house yourself? A good agent can be a valuable ally in your search for the right house, but there are some things you must understand. (These individuals are referred to by a number of names, including "salesperson," "broker," and "Realtor," the last of which refers to those who belong to the National Association of Realtors. In this book, we'll use the term "agent" to refer to all such real estate professionals.) The first is that real estate agents don't work for free, and their services will likely cost you a few thousand dollars. For that reason, a considerable number of home owners decide to sell their own homes. As you might imagine, the process takes considerable time and involves more than a little risk, but it is the way to go for about one home seller in ten.

Let's look at the pros and cons of each method of selling.

PROS AND CONS OF USING AN AGENT

While selling real estate can make for a highly profitable career, realty agents work hard for their money. For one thing, as commissioned agents, their income is directly related to the sales price of your house; the higher the price, the more money they earn. Moreover, if an agent fails to sell your house, he or she earns nothing at all.

At whatever price, an agent is responsible for dealing with

a seemingly endless array of hassles associated with home selling, from writing ads to showing the property on weekend after weekend to helping would-be buyers arrange financing. If you have no stomach for any of these kinds of activities, you will likely welcome the services of a competent agent.

On top of all this assistance they offer, agents usually are tapped into the regional or national network of people looking for homes like yours—the same number of bedrooms, in roughly the same location, at approximately the same price your home is worth. Many agents subscribe to a multiple listing service, which provides other agents with information about your home. (In fact, you should avoid working with an agent who doesn't subscribe to such a service.) In addition, agents will run advertisements for your house in local newspapers, at no cost to you. This access to prospective buyers can be extremely valuable. Not that you can't find buyers on your own—if you live in a desirable neighborhood, there may be no limit to the number of potential buyers for your home—but more often than not, such a ready supply of customers isn't available without an agent.

There's more an agent offers:

❑ A good agent will be familiar with the local mortgage market and local housing codes, helping you to avoid problems with your house that might make it difficult to sell.
❑ He or she will help you price your house in a fashion to bring you the most money without pricing it out of the local market.
❑ The agent will "prequalify" prospective buyers, ensuring that you don't waste a lot of time negotiating with individuals who don't have the means to complete a sale. (A truly top-notch agent will come complete with a prescreened list of potential buyers.)
❑ When someone makes an offer on your house, the agent will write it up in a binding contract, along with additional terms and conditions designed to protect your interests and facilitate the sale.
❑ He or she will help your buyer obtain financing.
❑ The agent will handle all the paperwork involved with closing the deal.

Some agents, particularly those associated with large national

real estate chains, offer additional services, such as a guaranteed sales plan, in which the agency will buy your house at a predetermined price if they can't sell it. Or, they may lend you the money for a down payment while you are waiting for your present home to sell. Some offer incentives to buyers, such as a warranty on the major appliances, or on one or more components of the house itself. The possibilities are limited only by the imagination of these firms' marketing and advertising gurus.

The biggest disadvantage of using a real estate agent, of course, is money: The agent's fee—typically 6 percent of the sales price—will run into the thousands of dollars. On a $75,000 house, that 6 percent commission equals $4,500; on a $120,000 house, it's $7,200. And when you consider that it usually isn't any more difficult to sell the $120,000 house than the $75,000 one, we're talking about picking up a nice piece of change for one's efforts.

It's always important to remember that while an agent represents your interests, he or she has his or her own interests in mind as well. And those interests may dictate that because the agent's child is about to get braces, your home needs to sell quickly rather than for top dollar. Such matters are difficult to prove, of course, but you must keep in mind that real estate agents are in business to sell houses, then move on to the next potential sale. The longer it takes to sell your property, the less profitable it will be for him or her to work with you.

Also keep in mind that when hiring an agent, you will need to give them the exclusive listing on it, usually for a period of ninety days. During that time, even if you sell the house to your best friend, the agent will receive the predetermined commission. And there is no assurance that the agent will work like a dog for you during that entire three-month period. Chances are that during the first few weeks, there will be a flurry of prospects marching through your living room, but if the house doesn't sell within that initial period, there will be a marked loss of enthusiasm—and a marked decrease in prospective buyers. In fact, some agents seem to disappear altogether during the final, nail-biting thirty days of the listing period if the first two months proved fruitless. Needless to say, that unproductive period will mean valuable time lost for you.

PROS AND CONS OF DOING IT YOURSELF

By selling your house yourself, you can put a lot of extra money in your pocket—money for which you probably could find some nice use. The fact is, with a little bit of insight and information, there isn't anything that a real estate agent does that you can't do yourself. We're talking about a pretty serious investment of time here, however, something a lot of folks simply don't have. But if you have more time than money, this may be the more profitable route to take.

Of course, this is easier said than done. All you need to do is examine the description of an agent's duties a few pages back and you'll see all that you'll need to do it yourself: Set the price, write and run the ads, locate prospective buyers, show the property, prescreen and qualify buyers, negotiate terms, handle the paperwork, and all the rest. Moreover, as an owner-seller, you may be offered lower prices—after all, the buyer knows that you're saving that 6 percent commission, and will likely try to offer at least that much less.

What may make the most sense is the best of all possible worlds: A real estate agent, working for a flat fee or reduced commission, helping you sell your house yourself. A number of flat-fee firms have sprouted up around the country, helping owner-sellers, some for about $1,000. Such firms provide signs, sample ads, forms, and some additional expertise. The services of discount brokers are somewhat more extensive, as are their rates, which typically range between $3,000 and $4,000. In either case, that's a lot less than you'd pay in commissions for a full-fledged agent ($1,000 would cover a 6 percent commission for a $16,667 house!).

Your decision to sell your own home will have a lot to do with the value of your time, but it will also be affected by local market conditions. Clearly, a seller's market—one in which there are fewer affordable homes in desirable neighborhoods than there are interested buyers—will make your job much easier. In fact, you probably shouldn't consider selling on your own unless there is a strong housing market and a favorable mortgage market—that is, rates aren't so high as to discourage potential buyers. Add to that a good, salable house in a decent location, and you may be a candidate for owner-selling.

Whether you use a flat-fee broker or go it alone, keep in mind that selling real estate is an extremely complex matter, involving a great deal of legalities and a lot of money. You should not embark on any real estate enterprise without a lot of information and professional support.

How to Choose an Agent

If you're like nine out of ten home sellers, you will eventually find an agent. (Even the majority of owner-sellers fail on their own, say the experts, eventually turning to professional help.) And choosing the right agent will be one of the most important decisions you make in the home-selling process.

How do you find a good real estate agent? Like finding any other service providers—from house cleaners to plumbers to dentists—it involves a combination of research and word of mouth. One means of finding someone familiar with your neighborhood is to scour the newspaper classified ads. As you read them for a week or so, you'll begin to see patterns: which agents specialize in a given part of town, or in certain types of houses.

Don't overlook the value of your own contacts in finding an agent. The best advice always comes from satisfied customers. Start by talking to friends, neighbors, relatives—and friends of friends, neighbors, and relatives—who may have recently bought or sold a home in the area in which you'll be buying or selling. What kind of service did they receive? Would they work with the agent again? If they had a good experience with the agent and would work with him or her again, there probably is no higher recommendation. You might also seek referrals from local lenders or a local attorney. If you're being transferred by your company, your company may be able to help in your search. Still another approach is to drive through the neighborhood, looking for SOLD signs. Those indicate a successful transaction, something you too are interested in. You might find out who listed the property, and what agent, if any, was involved in the sale.

An agent's qualifications are important, but you also want to find someone you like. After all, you may spend more than a few weekends with this person hanging out in your living room, waiting for prospective clients, or traipsing through your home at all sorts of inconvenient hours. And you want to find someone

who readily understands your needs, and will go out of his or her
way to get the best deal for you.

Some of the questions you might ask a prospective agent:

❑ Are you licensed? For how long?
❑ Are you a full- or part-time agent?
❑ Do you belong to a local, state, or national real estate associa-
tion?
❑ Does your firm participate in a multiple listing service?
❑ How many sales have you closed in the last three months?
❑ Can you help a prospective buyer find financing?
❑ How long have you worked as an agent in the area?
❑ What kind of marketing plan do you have for my house?

The answer to that last question—about the agent's knowledge
of the neighborhood—can be key. An agent who has worked in—
and, preferably, lived in—the neighborhood in which you're
looking will have firsthand knowledge of shopping, schools,
places of worship, building codes, tax rates, medical services,
city services, crime rates, and transportation services, and will
likely be able to sell prospective clients on the neighborhood's
virtues.

You should interview two or three active agents before
deciding on one. Each should give you a written analysis of the
local market, showing recent sales prices of comparable homes
in the area, including their asking prices and actual sales prices.
This analysis will be key to helping you and the agent arrive at
a realistic sales price. Don't automatically assume that the agent
who prices your house the highest will do the best job. It may be
that the high price is unreasonable for the market, and you may
waste several weeks advertising and showing the house at this
inflated price before you lower it to a more realistic level.

Besides qualifications, give high marks to the agent who is
enthusiastic and optimistic about selling your property. That
isn't necessarily the individual who talks the fastest, the loud-
est, or the longest. Rather, it might be the one who asks you a lot
of thoughtful questions and takes notes.

Don't be afraid to check references. By calling one to three
past clients of the agent, you will learn a lot from someone with

hindsight. These individuals may give you information on more than the agent in question; you may also receive some valuable tips about selling a house in your particular area, as well as some insight into pricing. Most of all, when calling references you should ascertain whether they were satisfied with the agent and whether they would do business with the agent again.

Should you go with a large firm or a small one? There are pros and cons to each. Some of the larger national firms have offices in every major city and can refer relocating clients from one city to an office in another. Clearly, this national access broadens your home's sales potential. But these larger firms may not give the same attention as smaller ones. Again, reputation and references are the best determining factor.

THE LISTING AGREEMENT

After you've selected an agent, you'll need to sign a listing agreement. This agreement will be the basis for your relationship with the agent. It will spell out the nature of the arrangement, how long it will last, and how much the agent will receive for selling your home. Remember: This will be a contractual obligation between you and the agent, so you should work out its terms very carefully.

There are several types of listing agreements:

❑ *The open listing* is a nonexclusive arrangement. It simply means that you will pay a commission to any agent who brings in a buyer who is ready, willing, and able to purchase your house; it also gives you the right to sell it yourself without paying a commission. An open listing may be given to any number of real estate agents. It is basically "first come, first served." For obvious reasons, real estate agents do not like open listings and likely will not spend much time and precious little money advertising and showing your property to clients. However, if your house is in an extremely desirable neighborhood and is in top-notch shape, and it is a buyer's market, you may not have a problem finding agents willing to bring clients your way. You may have to turn clients away.

❑ *The exclusive agency* listing gives a specific real estate agency

the right to sell your house. However, you still reserve the right to sell the property yourself without paying a commission. Again, because an agent may spend time and effort without being assured a commission, this is generally not preferred by most agents.

❏ *The exclusive right to sell* is the most common listing arrangement. It commits you to pay a commission to the agent, even if you sell the property yourself. This is the arrangement of choice for agents, who will have sufficient incentive to advertise your home and show it to as many potential clients as possible. Even if the house is sold by another agent—who finds the house advertised in the newspaper or the multiple listing service and brings a prospective buyer to see it—the listing agent will split the commission with the selling agent. (Usually, but not always: Some agents will not agree to split commissions.)

Forget everything you've heard about a "standard commission" of 6 or 7 percent or any other number. Nothing is standard; everything's negotiable. Real estate commissions are not set by law or established by any authority other than the individual agent or firm. True, a 6 percent (or whatever) commission may be the going rate in your area, but that still doesn't mean you'll have to pay that much. But don't necessarily count on it. It's a standard joke in the real estate business that all commissions are fully negotiable—from 6 percent up.

The bad news about agents is that they tend to be stubborn folk, and often won't budge on their "standard" commission. You may have to talk to a dozen or more firms before you'll find one to agree to sell your home for less than the going rate. But there are discount brokers out there, working for less than the so-called going rate. Keep in mind, however, that some of these brokers' *services* may also be discounted. That is, you may not get the same assistance you would from a full-fee, full-service broker. But then again, you may not need all of these services, so why pay top dollar?

In any case, the agents' commission will be spelled out in the listing agreement. Understand that this percentage is of the gross selling price. Any expenses you incur in the sale will likely

come out of your net proceeds. So, if you are listing with a 6 percent agent and the house sells for $100,000, but you are required to make $5,000 in repairs as one of the terms of sale, the agent's commission will be on the full $100,000, not on the actual amount you received after your fix-up expenses.

As for the listing period, it is typically ninety days, although it may range from between thirty days and one hundred-twenty days. It is in your interest to lock yourself in for the shortest possible period. For one thing, this will give the agent a great deal of incentive to get the property sold as quickly as possible. Moreover, if you're unhappy with the agent, the shorter listing period will allow you to find a more suitable one if your house remains unsold after the listing period.

GOING IT ALONE

As stated earlier, you needn't have a real estate agent to sell your home, but you will need some professional help if you try to sell on your own. (Such deals are often referred to as FSBO— pronounced *FIZZ-bo*—for "For Sale by Owner.") The sooner in the process you find such help the better.

One of the biggest problems facing FSBO sellers is separating feelings and the issue of money. After all, you've lived in this house for umpteen years and have some pretty good memories of it. It is very common for owner-sellers to let those emotions get in the way of a good deal. When acting as your own agent, it is crucial not to put your ego on the line. Don't become apoplectic if some prospective buyer doesn't like the rock garden you painstakingly created in the backyard, or doesn't appreciate the color scheme of the kitchen you labored over. Try to control your emotions and not let them get in the way of your ability to make wise decisions.

One of your first allies in the FSBO game will be a good lawyer. You should have an attorney on your team before you place a single advertisement or show it to even one prospective buyer. (With your luck, that first prospect will make you an offer, and without a lawyer you'll be unprepared to deal with it successfully.) The lawyer will show you the ins and outs of selling real estate, at least from a legal prospective. He or she won't turn you into a zillion-dollar-a-year salesperson, but you will learn

your rights and responsibilities when selling your property.

Among other things, the lawyer will help you draw up a sales contract that protects your interests and meets your particular needs. The lawyer also can serve as your escrow agent: When an offer is made, the escrow agent holds onto the earnest money until settlement. In short, you lawyer will be your friend and guiding light throughout the FSBO process. Not any old lawyer will do. The one who drew up your will or handled your divorce won't necessarily be well versed in the fine points of real estate transactions. In other words, don't just find any lawyer; find a qualified one.

Do not take this advice lightly: Get a good lawyer. Using forms that you can purchase in a stationery store or photocopy from a do-it-yourself book just won't cut it in the big, bad world of real estate. You'll be gambling away your hard-earned equity.

Chapter 3
Getting It In Shape

If you had to choose between a house that looked great and one that didn't, which would *you* choose? Chances are you'd go for the property that looked as if it had been taken care of, even if you planned to repaint and make substantial changes in it before you moved in. You'd be amazed how much even a little bit of cleaning and painting can help sell a house. And you'd be equally amazed at how many sellers fail to make even the most basic efforts to spruce up their houses before trying to sell them..

Of course, your house may need more than a bit of sprucing up to put it in top-notch condition. If your home is typical, there's plenty of loose plaster, sagging boards, gouged wood, dripping faucets, and cracked pavement to keep your basic home handyman (or -woman) occupied for a month of Sundays. You'll have to be the judge of whether or not to invest the time and money to get these things in shape before putting your home on the market.

You might want to start by asking a few friends over to take a good hard look at your house. Ask them to be as critical as possible, and let them have the run of the house for a couple of hours. Don't be embarrassed to show your house's warts: Only homes on *Lifestyles of the Rich and Famous* don't have a few things wrong with them. Your friends' evaluations will give you a good idea of how strangers might see your home—and what might turn them off to buying it.

Real estate agents often speak of "curb appeal." That refers to how your house looks from the curb—you know, when a couple goes out for a weekend drive to look at houses, eliminating a lot of prospects without even getting out of the car. So, it's important that your house look as good as possible from the outside. Again, your critical friends might come in handy, stepping across the street to evaluate the first impression given by your house: The

yard, any junk piled around, the condition of the house itself. For prospective home buyers, those first impressions will be lasting.

How Buyers See Your House

When people shop for a home, they tend to look at a lot of properties. So, whether they're looking with a real estate agent or by themselves, buyers tend to get pretty good at figuring out the good and not-so-good aspects of potential properties. You should examine your house in this same way. It will give you a good overview of potential problems that may be pointed out by prospective buyers, and will also provide some insight into your house's extras (or lack thereof) that may affect your initial asking price. You might want to conduct this inspection with a note pad, jotting down good and bad points to which you can later refer when determining what you'll need to fix before selling (bad points), and writing an ad after everything's in shipshape (good points).

At first glance, a buyer will consider four key aspects of the property:

❑ Whether it offers the space, layout, and features they need.
❑ The desirability of the neighborhood and location.
❑ The important faults or defects that may create problems for them now or later on.
❑ How much it will cost them to own and maintain.

Buyers likely will not be concerned quite yet with the structure and mechanical systems of the house. For now, they're only giving the property a once over for livability. Here are some of the first things they'll want to consider:

❑ Is the floor plan well laid out, with separate areas for working, living, and sleeping?
❑ Are the rooms large enough to accommodate their possessions?
❑ Is the traffic pattern appropriate for their family? Where and how will children enter? Will the dining room get used as a hallway?
❑ Are the kitchen appliances relatively up to date? Are there the

ones they need, including a dishwasher and disposal? Is it laid out appropriately, with workable storage, cooking, and cleanup areas? Is there adequate counter, cabinet, and storage space?
❑ Are eating areas convenient to the kitchen?
❑ Is there adequate storage, including a garage, if necessary?
❑ Is there an adequate yard to accommodate their lifestyle, children, and pets?
❑ Are there enough bathrooms—both full bathrooms (those with bath or shower) and half bathrooms (those without)? Are they located where needed most?
❑ Does the house *feel* right?

Doing Your Own Inspection

To be an effective seller, you have to put yourself in the buyer's shoes. For buyers, the key rule is to

❑ open
❑ close
❑ look into
❑ look behind and
❑ operate

everything. Buyers want to look for hidden flaws, cracks, blemishes, and defects, as well as the less-hidden things. If the house is on the market for sale, it is there to be inspected.

So, to be fully armed, you should do your own thorough inspection. You want to get a reasonably good fix on how much money it will cost you to remedy any and all problems.

Let's start at the bottom and work our way up.

Outside the House
❑ *Foundation, grading, and drainage.* Check for holes, cracks, or unevenness. Are there any cracks or porous areas in the foundation walls? Is the floor even? Water is a house's worst enemy. If there is not proper drainage, water will build up in and around the house, causing severe damage to its structure. Settlement causes some water problems: Some homes have what builders call negative pitch, a common phenomenon even among newer

homes, where fluffed-up soil subsides over time and surface water runs back toward the house. Look at the outside ground to make sure it slopes away from the house. If water doesn't lead away from the house, it will make its way inside.

❑ *Driveway and sidewalks.* Again, you should be looking for holes and cracks. Are the surfaces near the house—the driveway, walkway, patios, and sidewalks—in good condition, or must they be resurfaced?

❑ *Grounds.* Aside from its size, is the land in good shape? If it appears eroded or contains sunken portions, it may indicate a drainage problem. Is there enough topsoil for planting new grass (about five inches), shrubs (at least eighteen inches), and trees (at least two feet)? If the frontyard or backyard are not well taken care of, it may provide an indication of the general wear and tear on the house. If there are fences, look for holes, loose or missing sections, or rotted posts.

The lawn, both in front and back, should be well manicured. It may be worth the investment to have a professional gardener give it a good once over, pulling weeds and trimming shrubbery, especially if it keeps light out of the house. You might add a dose of fertilizer to "green up" the lawn and mulch in flower beds and around trees. If necessary, reseed or resod thin areas.

❑ *Critters and pests.* These can range from rats to termites to a long list of tiny little things that can take up residence in a house or environs, any of which could make life less than rosy. Termites are one of the biggest pests, but you probably won't see any obvious signs of infestation unless you're a trained professional.

❑ *Outside steps.* These can be another sign of a bad foundation, improper drainage, or otherwise shaky ground. When a house settles or shifts, the outside steps often don't move with it, leaving gaps between steps, or between the steps and the house. And once they do separate, there is great potential for water problems, as water gets into the cracks, then freezes and thaws.

❑ *Brick work.* Again, look for cracks and loose or missing mortar.

If there's a chimney, look for loose or missing bricks. Obviously, the chimney, when seen from outside, shouldn't be tilting.

❏ *Outside appearance.* If the house has siding—clapboards, shingles, or other materials—look for loose or missing pieces, lifting, or warping. If it's painted, look for peeling, chipping, or blistering. A fresh coat of paint probably is the best remedy for a less-than-stunning exterior. An alternative is to paint only the front shutters and window frames. Gutters and downspouts, which are prone to peeling paint, are other items that look especially good when freshly painted. If you have a painted front fence, that too is another prime candidate for making a postitive impression on potential buyers.

❏ *Front door.* The nicer it looks, the more impressive the whole house will appear. It should be freshly cleaned and painted. And the walkway leading up to it should be clean enough to eat from! Invest in a new welcome mat and make sure your doorbell is working. If the hinges squeak, apply oil or WD-40 lubricant.

❏ *Gutters and downspouts.* Aside from the aforementioned paint, check for missing sections, gaps, or holes in the joints. Gutters and downspouts should remove all water at least two feet from the house itself. Look for signs that water may be running down the side of the house, indicating that gutters or spouts are blocked or broken.

❏ *Outside lighting.* Is there adequate lighting in the front and back to provide both illumination and security?

❏ *Garage.* Check the doors, roof, siding, and windows. You should keep the garage door closed at all possible times. Even the neatest, most organized garage is best kept out of public view. Ideally, you should clear the garage of everything except cars and tools, which should be hung from hooks on the walls or placed on shelves. This may be a good time to hold a garage sale.

❏ *Roof.* These need to be repaired or replaced several times during the lifetime of a house, so it's important to know the kind

of roofing used and its condition. The life expectancy of roofing depends on the material:

asphalt rolls	10 years
built-up roofing	10-20 years
wood shingles	10-40 years
asphalt shingles	15-20 years
asphalt interlocking shingles	15-25 years
metal roofing	15-40 years
clay tiles	20+ years
asphalt multi-thickness shingles	20-30 years
asbestos cement shingles	30-75 years
slate shingles	30-100 years

Check to see whether the existing roof includes a warranty that may be transferred to the buyer.

❑ *Trash*. Needless to say, there shouldn't be any.

Keep in mind that it is your decision ultimately as to how much, if any, of the information you find in this inspection you will reveal to the buyer. Honesty usually is the best policy, of course, but reveal what you feel is appropriate.

INSIDE THE HOUSE
So much for the outside. Now, let's go inside and take a look around. Again, we'll start at the bottom and work our way up.

❑ *Basement*. Any part of the house that's below ground is subject to leaking, and a leaky house is not something buyers want to fool around with; it's one of the most serious problems of home ownership. Ideally, you should check this out right after a heavy rainstorm, enabling you to inspect for leaks and seepage.

What are the signs of a leaky basement? You'll have to use your basic senses: It will smell or look feel damp. You'll probably notice the musty smell as soon as you enter the basement. You'll see stains, streaks, or spots on the walls and floor. You might find loose tiles or warped flooring. And if it's bad enough, it will simply *feel* damp.

Don't just take a cursory look around. Buyers will likely look under and behind things, and move large objects that might be hiding evidence of leakiness. They may be suspicious if the basement is freshly painted: It could indicate that you're trying to hide something. If you do clean the basement before a potential buyer visits, make sure it doesn't retain the just-cleaned odor of Pinesol or some other cleaning substance; that could be another telltale sign of a cover-up.

❏ *Utilities.* Take a look at the key mechanical components, including the water heater, the heating and air conditioning systems, the water supply, and the electrical system.

The *water heater* should be large enough for family use. For a family of three, that means at least fifty gallons; if it is larger, at least sixty-five gallons. It should be well insulated, as should the pipes going out of it carrying hot water throughout the house. A timer, enabling it to cycle on during the day and off at night, is recommended. The water heater shouldn't show any signs of leaks or rust.

The *plumbing* isn't easy to check if you're not an expert, but you should do a superficial inspection for leaks and rust. Try all the toilets and sinks, particularly those on the top floor if it's a multilevel house. You might try running several sinks or flushing several toilets at once, to see how much that affects water pressure. It should have some effect, but it shouldn't reduce water flow to a trickle. If the water pressure isn't good, there's a decent chance there's a big plumbing job on the horizon. Look also for clogged or sluggish drains and dripping faucets. Get any leaky faucets fixed.

The *heating system* is an important item for today's buyers. A bad one can be a money burner if it's not efficient or adequate. The fuel source is one factor. In most parts of the country, natural gas is the least expensive energy source, followed by oil and electricity. But even if yours is an all-electric home, it may be well-insulated and contain energy-saving features such as a heat pump.

The best indicator of an efficient system, of course, is to show prospective buyers a year's worth of utility bills—electricity, oil, and gas, as appropriate. The more you can document your home's energy efficiency, the easier it will be to sell.

The *electrical system* is another behind-the-walls network that can be costly to overhaul. In general, the older the house, the more likely it is to carry inadequate electrical service. Prospective buyers will be interested to know the amperage, an indication of the system's ability to carry an assortment of kitchen appliances, a washer and dryer, TVs, stereos, VCRs, clocks, reading lamps, electric toothbrushes, and hair dryers. Most homes require at least 100-amp service. If the house has central air conditioning, make that 200 amps. Many houses built before the mid-1950s, unless they have been upgraded, carry only 60 amps of service.

Another major concern of buyers is aluminum wiring, which was commonly used in houses built between 1965 and 1973. In recent years, aluminum wiring has been found to be a major fire hazard, causing the federal government to declare it an "imminent hazard" in more than a million and a half homes. (Aluminum wiring installed after 1973 isn't considered to be a problem.) The fire hazard stems from the way aluminum wiring of that period was connected to outlets and switches, causing them to overheat. If you have such wiring you are strongly advised to have it repaired or replaced. If you're not sure about the kind of wiring you have and the house was built during that period, it would be a good idea to have an independent housing inspector or electrician examine it.

The *air conditioning* system, if there is one, should be large enough to cool the entire house. It should work quietly and efficiently and, ideally, should have a high energy efficiency rating. This will be difficult for a buyer to check unless he or she is able to visit the house during the dog days of summer. Again, an examination of actual bills is the best thing to show buyers.

FLOORS, WALLS, WINDOWS, AND DOORS
A buyer needn't be a carpenter to appreciate good craftsman-

ship. One needs only to use one's instincts. Therefore, you should evaluate the house the way a smart buyer would.

❑ *Floors* should feel solid. Jump up and down on them a couple of times. Does the floor give a little or remain firm? Most floors, particularly in older homes, seem to creak a little, so this isn't a problem unless it is excessive and widespread. Look for the levelness of floors, as well as bowing, movement, and looseness when you walk around. Also check their surface condition. Are wooden floorboards cracked, stained, or loose? Are linoleum tiles discolored or missing? Are bathroom tiles in good shape?

Carpeted areas should be professionally cleaned, especially if you have dogs, cats, or other pets. You may be able to get by with sprinkling on carpet deodorant or scrubbing carpets with water mixed with vinegar or soda. Dry out the carpets as quickly as possible lest they become mildewed; use a fan or hair dryer if necessary.

❑ *Walls.* A coat of paint is one of the cheapest and most profitable home improvements you can make. It may cost you a few hundred dollars, but it may add several thousand dollars to your home's value. Choose the color carefully. White, off-white, cream and other neutral colors are best. Light colors tend to open up rooms, giving them an airy feeling.

❑ *Doors* should open and close with ease. While there may be some seasonal stickiness due to summer humidity or winter dryness, no door should require strenuous pulling. Your can of WD-40 will come in handy: use it to quiet squeaks and loosen up stiff hinges. Also check the condition of screens or glass panels that may not be installed due to the time of year. Don't forget locks: Are they adequate for your safety and comfort? Do all outside locks require the same key, or are several keys needed to open the front, back, side, and garage doors? What about storm doors? In colder parts of the country, these can go a long way toward saving energy.

❑ *Windows* should be in good repair, with frames freshly painted. All windows should have blinds, shutters, or curtains. When

possible, hang a plant in front of a window with an otherwise unappealing view. In general, keep shades and blinds open, letting in as much light as possible. Most buyers are turned off by darkened rooms.

Keep in mind that windows are one of the biggest energy wasters in a house if they're inadequate or poorly fitting. Indeed, about two thirds of all heat loss in houses is through windows and doors. Most older houses have single-paned windows, which may be inadequate for today's energy costs; the price of installing double-paned windows (two thicknesses of glass with a small air space in between) or storm windows (a second window installed outside the first) is not inexpensive, but it may pay off over time in reduced fuel bills and, of course, will provide greater comfort in keeping heat in during the winter and out during the summer.

Check details: Are the windows cracked, scratched, or broken? Are the screens in good condition? (If it's winter, they might not be installed.) You can't adequately check windows without testing them. Even if they appear in good condition, the sashes or frames may be warped or broken, leaking in cold air (or, in summer, hot air) and water. Do they open and close with ease? Do their locking mechanisms work well? Are the locks decent enough for your comfort and security?

The Rest of the House

❑ *Insulation.* You should be aware of the amount and type of insulation in your house's ceilings and walls. This will probably not be an easy task—after all, the insulation is behind the walls and ceiling. But you should be able to provide prospective buyers with some indication of insulation, ideally expressed as an "R" factor, a standardized term that describes a wall or ceiling's resistance to hot and cold air passing through. For example, in the cold Midwest, a house ideally should have R-19 insulation, the equivalent of about four inches of fiberglass in the ceiling.

Because heat rises, the most important insulation is in the attic or, if there's no attic, between the top floor and the roof. In most parts of the country, you'll need about a foot of insulation, offering an energy efficiency rating of between R-22 and R-30. There are a host of other energy-saving measures, from sealing up door jambs to covering hot-water pipes to the aforementioned

storm windows and doors. The idea is that the tighter a house is sealed against escaping air, the less energy it will waste.

But it shouldn't be *too* tight. It's important that a house be able to "breathe," lest it build up humidity, odors, pollutants and, in the summer, heat. In the rush to save energy, overly tight houses can result in anything from structural damage to poor health for their occupants.

❏ *Kitchen*. You may not be surprised to learn that the kitchen is the most important room and the one most scrutinized by the majority of buyers. And with good reason: there is much in it that affects livability, and so much that must jibe with individuals' habits and lifestyles.

No matter what kind of kitchen you have, the key word here is *clean*. Every nook and cranny should shine and all those layers of grease and grime (which you probably hadn't noticed in years) must be cleansed away. A professional cleaning is probably the best bet, someone who will get those spots you've long forgotten about. Don't miss a thing: The insides of the refrigerator and oven should be spotless, as should the stove's ventilating hood. Consider relining the cabinets and pantry shelves. Eliminate as much clutter as possible from the countertops.

Aside from having it spotlessly clean, having an up-to-date kitchen is important. Ideally, a kitchen will have:

- ✔ adequate counter space
- ✔ adequate cabinet space
- ✔ good layout
- ✔ good ventilation (including a window over the sink)
- ✔ modern appliances (including dishwasher and garbage disposal)
- ✔ adequate electrical outlets
- ✔ a sizable pantry
- ✔ modern flooring
- ✔ a bright and sunny feel

❏ *Bathrooms*. These are the next most important rooms in a house, at least as far as attractiveness to buyers is concerned. Tiny, plain bathrooms—the kind found in most older houses—

stand out like a sore thumb. Buyers will want to know the following: Is there adequate privacy, from both the inside and out? Are the bathroom appliances shiny and modern, or are there stains and cracks in the sink and tub? Are the wall and floor tiles intact, or are they loose, chipped, cracked, or missing? Is there adequate counter and cabinet space? Proper ventilation? As with the kitchen, this will be a highly subjective determination.

Again, the watchword here is cleanliness. Bathrooms should be spotless and smelling as fresh as possible. (Those inexpensive stick-on-the-wall fresheners work well.) Tiles should be scrubbed and grouted if necessary. Use vinegar to rub away hard-water spots and soap scum from chrome accessories. Replace the shower curtain, or at least the liner, as well as dirty bath mats. Hang up some colorful towels. And unclog all drains.

❑ *Bedrooms*. Simply put, the more the better, and the bigger the better. Most buyers want enough rooms for the occupants—parents, children, etc.—as well as visiting family and friends. Check also for closet space: To be a fully qualified bedroom, it should have enough space for nearby storage so that its occupant(s) needn't go down the hall to get dressed. The location of bedrooms is important, too. Ideally, they should be far enough away from the family's general living space to provide adequate privacy.

❑ *Living room*. Its adequacy will have a lot to do with how much one entertains and whether there is another room—a family room, rec room, or den, for example—in which a family will do the bulk of its TV-watching, reading, and conversing. If the living room has a fireplace, you should check it carefully. Does the damper work? Has the chimney been cleaned out recently? (It probably hasn't; very few sellers consider doing this to enhance a home's resale value.) If the fireplace is clean and attractive, make it the focal point of the room. Buy an attractive set of fireplace tools and set some firewood nearby in a pretty basket.

❑ *Storage*. Having a lot of storage space is either a necessity or

a luxury, depending on your particular lifestyle. In any case, having adequate storage is a big plus for buyers. These needn't be enormous spaces, and you can accomplish a lot simply by cleaning out your closets! (This is a wise thing to do in any case before you move.) There's nothing less appealing than opening a closet and finding it filled with junk. Strive for a clean, uncluttered look. Again, a yard sale may be in order.

❑ *Other amenities.* Make sure you make it perfectly clear to prospective buyers what comes with the house—and what doesn't. Does that full-length mirror in the bedroom remain? How about the living room drapes? Do all the appliances convey to the buyer, or does that auxiliary freezer in the garage go with you? A full inventory of items should be included in the purchase contract, but for now, you should be aware of exactly what you are selling.

SELLING YOUR HOUSE AS IS

You may decide after this inspection that there are simply too many problems to worry about. Rather than spending a lot of time and money fixing things up, you might conclude it's wisest to just lower the selling price a few thousand dollars and sell the house as is.

Fine. You absolutely have the right to do this. But be aware that you are being penny-wise and pound-foolish: the additional amount you will likely receive for your fixed-up house may be more than the money you would save by leaving things as is. In other words, the improvements will more than pay for themselves through an increased sales price. Buyers like homes that look ready to move into (regardless of whether they repaint and decorate before moving in). Among other things, it assures them that the house was well taken care of—even if the bulk of the "care" you gave your house took place primarily during the final weeks before selling it. It's a psychological advantage to have things in good repair, and you probably will sell you house much more quickly if you do.

THE VALUE OF MAKING IMPROVEMENTS

So much for getting your home in shape. But what about adding

to it? Is it possible to enhance the value of your home by adding a few amenities, the cost of which could more than pay itself back in the increased sales price?

Maybe, but probably not. According to data compiled by *Remodeling* magazine, home improvements don't pay for themselves fully at resale. In fact, as the table below shows, none of the eleven improvements surveyed paid for themselves at resale. (These figures are based on national averages and will vary from area to area.)

RATING THE RETURN ON HOME IMPROVEMENTS

Project	Cost	Average return at resale (%)
Major kitchen remodel	$20,641	88 %
Bath addition	10,151	85
Minor kitchen remodel	7,892	84
Master suite	21,074	79
Family room addition	31,223	78
Replace siding	7,789	74
Bath remodel	7,568	73
Deck addition	5,109	67
Sun room addition	15,368	61
Replace windows	6,577	57
Replace doors	1,541	42

Reprinted from the October 1989 issue of *Remodeling* magazine. © 1989, Hanley-Wood, Inc.

As you can see, home improvements are most effective only if you are planning to stick around for a few more years to enjoy them yourself. Otherwise, you'll be wasting your money—not to mention enduring a lot of construction woes.

So, now your house is in topnotch shape—or as close to that as it will ever be—and it's time to get down to the business of actually finding a buyer.

To Market, To Market

Even if your house is a dream come true—immaculate, in fine shape, in a great location, with a great price—you won't do it justice if the house isn't marketed properly. If you work with a real estate agent, some of this responsibility will fall on that person's shoulders. But because no one knows your house as well as you do, and because real estate agents tend to market all houses in pretty much the same way, you'll need to take an active role in the process, so that you find as many prospective buyers as possible as quickly and efficiently as you can.

One important factor that will determine how much marketing is necessary is whether you are selling in a buyer's market (when there are more houses for sale than available buyers and demand is low) or a seller's market (when there are fewer homes than buyers and demand is high). Obviously, when demand is high, your efforts will be somewhat easier; you might even be able to advertise your home via word of mouth. But you can succeed even in a buyer's market, if you play your cards right.

ESTABLISHING AN ASKING PRICE
Figuring out how much your house is worth on the open market involves as much art as science. The first step, in any case, involves some homework.

First and foremost, you must know your house—really know it—its good points and its bad points. Go over your inspection checklist and note the problem areas. Assume that the buyer will have a similar list, so the better prepared you are, the less the chance you'll encounter any surprises. You might obtain an estimate of how much it will cost to remedy any problems, in case your making these repairs becomes part of the negotiations.

You will also be well served by having a list of "comparables." These are examples of recent sales prices of comparable

homes within a mile of the house you are selling; the closer they are to your home, the better. A "comparable" house needn't be exactly like yours. But it should have roughly the same square feet and number of bedrooms and be about the same age, give or take a few years. Keep in mind that some seemingly identical houses a few blocks away may be worth different amounts due to a variety of factors, from the type of construction to the availability of on-street parking. To make the comparisons among different properties meaningful, it may be helpful to translate the sales prices into dollars per square foot. For example, a 1,450-square-foot house that sold for $80,000 cost $55.17 per square foot ($80,000 divided by 1,450). It would also be helpful to know the difference between their listing prices and actual sales prices; a local real estate agent may have this information handy.

To get the best comparisons possible, you should attend some local open houses, comparing others' homes—and asking prices—with yours. By walking through these homes yourself, you'll get a good feel for how the living space and amenities stack up against those of your home. You might even pick up a few tips about home-selling techniques.

Another ready reference is local classified ads. A thorough reading will give you a good sense of what the asking prices are in your area; remember, these aren't necessarily the actual *sales* prices. Still, this information will help you determine the range of what people think they can get for their homes.

In the end, it comes down to the simple matter of picking a price. Don't be greedy, but don't underprice your home. Keep in mind that while the asking price will likely come down somewhat, it probably won't ever go up. So your asking price should be somewhat on the high side, but not so high as to scare off potential buyers.

GETTING IT APPRAISED

The best evidence of a home's worth is a professional appraisal. If you are selling your home yourself, this is essential. It will cost you between $100 and $200 for this service, but it may pay for itself by placing an "official" value on your home. (If you are selling your home through a real estate agent, you may not need this. The agent will price the home on the basis of comparable homes in the area, and because it is being listed by a professional

agent, prospective buyers will have less reason to question the basis for your asking price.) To find an appraiser, ask local lenders or real estate agents. To ensure that the appraisal will meet top professional standards, seek an appraiser who is a member of either the Society of Real Estate Appraisers or the American Institute of Real Estate Appraisers.

FINDING YOUR MARKET

Who would buy your home? "Anyone with a lot of sense," you might answer, and that's not a bad start. But you've got to get somewhat more specific. Consider for a moment your house's location, size, price, and other characteristics. Think about the following:

❑ Will it appeal more to a younger buyer or an older one?
❑ Will it appeal more to an upscale buyer or a downscale one?
❑ Is it suitable for a large family or a small one?
❑ What kind of people would like the house?
❑ What did you like about the house when you bought it?

This is the kind of thinking you should do to pinpoint prospective buyers. The answers you get should help you locate them and appeal to them through an advertisement. For example:

❑ *Older people* might be concerned primarily with matters of security and health. They might gravitate to low-maintenance ranch-style homes, probably under 1,500 square feet. Single-story homes with no stairs and easy access are also desirable.
❑ *Single people* generally prefer an environment in which it is easy to meet other singles through social or recreational activities. Safety is also a consideration for those who live alone.
❑ *Young childless couples* will likely be looking for an affordable house that offers room to grow. They might not be as concerned about being on a busy street as would a family with young children.
❑ *Families with children* will have a longer list of concerns, from good schools to safety to access to shopping and recreational facilities. A fenced-in yard also may be key.

The price of your home, of course, will also define the market. If your home is priced in the low range for your area, you are likely

to get a lot of younger couples and other economy-minded buyers who are looking for an affordable first home. Slightly more upscale buyers might be looking for a place in which to grow; they might move in with designs for renovating or adding extra space. Those more upwardly mobile status-seekers might be attracted to a quality home that needs little or no work; quality and a prestigious address may be uppermost in their minds. Those among the upper crust will focus on a variety of factors, from location to construction quality. By considering all such matters, you'll have a better feel for whom you are trying to attract, which will better enable you to take the next step: writing an ad.

How to Write an Ad

So you've got a great house, all dressed up with nowhere to go. Welcome to the wonderful world of hype.

Selling a house is simple. No matter what its condition, there's *someone* out there who wants it and is willing to pay a fair price for it. The problem is finding that person. That's where salesmanship comes in. What's important when marketing your house to others is a single cardinal rule: Every house has its good points. Discover what they are and feature them in your sales pitch.

You may find this difficult to believe. What could possibly be attractive, you're saying, about a tiny fifty-year-old one-bedroom stucco house with leaky pipes and more than a few walls that need repainting, sitting cheek-by-jowl against the new Interstate? Well, your house could be a "handyman's special" or "a great starter home" for first-time buyers. The point is, whatever its age, whatever its condition, there's something good about your house, something that will appeal to some buyer out there. Your job will be to determine who that special someone is, and where he or she may be lurking.

But first, you must evaluate your merchandise. Finding the "good points" of some houses takes a little creativity, to be sure. But it can be done. For example:

❏ Is it on a busy street, smack in the middle of a shopping area, with big, clunky buses streaming past throughout the day and night? Let the world know that it's "close to shopping," "convenient to transportation," "a commuter's dream," and "in-town living."

❏ Is it far, far away from everything, miles from the nearest school, store, gas station, or public transportation? Call it "off the beaten path" with "a picturebook setting."
❏ Is it small and basic? Call it "a great buy for newlyweds." Does it have odd-shaped rooms and a sort of eclectic feel? Say it is "something different," whatever that means.

Imitation, as they say, is the sincerest form of flattery. Begin your ad-writing campaign by scouring the classifieds in your local paper. Read the descriptions of homes for sale and try to determine which ads get your attention. Is it the one with the bold headline? Are there certain key words that attract you? Is it location? Price? Mark the cream of the crop and take a few minutes to analyze what makes them good.

Don't be cavalier about writing your ad. According to one source, more than three-fourths of all home buyers checked newspaper ads before buying. But more is not necessarily better: You needn't advertise three, four, or five times a week to get results. One or two weekends' worth may be all you need.

There is an art to writing classified ads. How else could you cram so much information into so few words? You're paying by the word or line, so you'll have to say it fast and say it well. The idea is simple: You want to give potential buyers enough information to make them want to investigate further. Short, sweet, and to the point is the best approach. Use bright, exciting-sounding terms that will make your house sound appealing.

Start off with a great headline. If you've already read a few columns of classifieds, you'll know exactly what this means. The headline must grab readers' attention and get them into the body of the ad. Be creative. By having figured out your house's good points, you should be ready to create that great opening line. Here are some classics for inspiration:

Affordably Priced	Immaculate Condition
City Chic	Light & Lovely
Convenience Plus	Live in Style
Country Living	Loaded with Charm
Cozy and Affordable	Location Plus
Exclusive	Minutes from Everything
Gorgeous	Move-In Condition
Hurry!	Owner Must Sell

Priced to Sell	Value Plus
Stop Looking	Walk to Work
Unbelievable!	Won't Last the Weekend

Note that not all of these statements mean something. They're intended primarily to invoke a feeling. Some classics ("Priced to Sell") are almost laughable (how else would you have priced your house?), but they are used again and again because they seem to work. The more headlines you read, the more you'll start to find some key words for your own ad.

So much for the headline. Now for the rest of the ad. According to one survey, more than three-fourths of all readers of real estate ads look for location before everything else. If your house is in an extremely desirable location, you might consider this when writing the headline. Is it close to schools, shopping, downtown? Is it in the lively city, quiet suburbs, lazy country?

Also of obvious importance is price. If you read other classifieds, you'll find that asking price often is part of the headline, or at least is featured near the top of the ad. You've got to remember that sometimes people skim hundreds of classifieds, looking for the two or three that might fit their needs. House hunters don't take the time to read through every ad, so if you don't give them the information they need right away, they may move on to the next ad.

You might want to list the actual asking price, or you might prefer to be a bit more elusive, such as stating "lower 60s," meaning that the price is in the $60,000 to $65,000 range. Readers will respond to a home that sounds appealing on paper, even if they don't really know the price. However, you want to give enough price information that you screen out potential buyers who can't afford your house; otherwise, you'll get needless calls from people who aren't really bona fide prospects.

Another important piece of information is housing style— the number of stories and the type of house. Words like "colonial," "rambler," "Cape Cod," "Victorian," and "townhouse" are common; if you're not sure how to describe your house, you might want to check with a lender or agent. If it's nondescript, you might want to skirt the issue, using such words as "modern," "classic," or "contemporary." Even more vague but commonly used are such adjectives as "sunny," "cozy," "delightful," "glorious," "lovely," and on and on.

Next come your home's features, and here is where you will bump up against the limits of advertising space. Of course, you must give the important facts—numbers of bedrooms and bathrooms, for example, but you also must give some tantalizing details. Obviously, you won't be able to mention *every* charming aspect of your home, so you'll have to pick those few things that might help your property stand out from the crowd. If, in the previous chapter, you inspected your home with pencil and paper and inventoried all its assets and liabilities, you may have the basis for picking and choosing. Some of the things you should highlight:

❑ central air conditioning (if that's important in your part of the country)
❑ decks, porches, patios
❑ finished basement
❑ fireplace
❑ garage (particularly if it accommodates more than one car)
❑ modern and fully equipped kitchen
❑ outstanding view
❑ recreation room
❑ wall-to-wall carpeting

Of course, you'll want to mention all these things in good old classified advertising code. Here are some abbreviations commonly used in ads:

A/C	air conditioning
ac	acre
appl	appliances
assum	assumable mortgage
BA	bathroom
bal	balcony
blt	built-in
BR	bedroom
brk	brick
bsmt	basement
bth	bath
burg/fire	burglar/fire alarm
CAC	central air conditioning
con	convenient to

ctr	center
dbl	double
DR	dining room
dk	deck
EIK (or eat-in)	eat-in kitchen
fam rm	family room
FHA	qualifies for FHA financing
fin	finished
flr	floor
fml	formal
fpl	fireplace
gar	garage
gas	gas heating
ingrnd	in-ground pool
in-law	separate apartment
lib	library
lg	large
lndry	laundry room
lo	low
loc	location
LR	living room
md's	maid's room
mint	excellent condition
mod	modern
mstr	master bedroom
mtg	mortgage
nr	near
occup	occupancy
pnld	paneled
prfl off	professional office
pkg	parking
pvt	private
rec rm	recreation room
rm	room
schls	schools
scpd	landscaped
semi-det	semi-detached
sep ent	separate entrance
shwr	shower
sld dr	sliding doors
spklr	underground sprinkler system

starter	small first home
steam	steam heating
terr	terrace
TH	townhouse
txs	taxes
VA	qualifies for VA financing
w/	with
WW cpt	wall-to-wall carpeting
wbf	wood-burning fireplace
xtr	extras
yd	yard

If you've made significant improvements, they are worth mentioning: refinished floors, freshly painted walls, new carpeting, refinished kitchen, etc. And if you are selling the house yourself—that is, without a real estate agent—you probably should mention this. People are seduced by the prospect of saving money from an owner-sold house. When listing your phone number, however, you should be specific as to times people should call, lest you be pestered at odd hours. You'd be surprised how early on Sunday mornings some people read the classifieds. *But under no circumstances should you include your actual address in the ad.*

Here are a few additional suggestions for writing effective ads:

❏ *Don't Overabbreviate.* You've probably seen ads chock-full of acronyms and funny words, usually in an attempt to fit the most information into the least space. For example:

DWNTWN—lg. 2 br, 1.5 ba, lr, dr, cac, fin bsmt, pkg, nr shops, extras. Lovely. $86K. 555-4312.

You've got to admit that this ad (a large, two-bedroom, one-and-a-half bathroom house, with living room, dining room, central air conditioning, a finished basement, parking, located downtown near shopping, with other amenities—and of course it's lovely—for which the seller is asking $86,000) is a bit too sketchy to get through easily. A house shopper, eyes already partially glazed from browsing the classifieds, might simply skip over this one because it's too difficult to decipher.

❑ *Don't Be Vague.* The other side of the coin, of course, is giving too little information. Consider this ad:

> DWNTWN—lg. lovely house, great kitchen. Nr shop, must see to apprec. By owner. $86,000. 555-4312

This ad may be a bit too short, sweet, and to the point. While it's good to know that the house is lovely, has a great kitchen, and is near shopping, it's even better to know a few other things—such as whether there are any bedrooms or bathrooms, for starters. A few additional facts would help here.

❑ *Don't Underabbreviate.* This will benefit no one except the owners of the newspaper in which you advertise. Keep it short and simple.

OTHER WAYS TO ADVERTISE

The classifieds, however popular, aren't the only way to advertise your house. There are a couple other sources that will cost you little or nothing.

❑ *Your Front Yard.* The most obvious place is outside the house itself. Lawn signs (or window signs for those without front yards) can attract the attention of people already in the neighborhood. Don't overlook them as potential buyers: Some of them may be renters in search of something nearby to own; others might be looking for something a bit bigger—or even a bit smaller.

Unless you are ready and willing to show your home—or at least talk about it—at almost any hour of the day or night, your sign should include the notation BY APPOINTMENT ONLY. This is true even if your home is being shown exclusively by a real estate agent (whose name and phone number should be prominently displayed on the sign), since some people will still assume that your home is perpetually open and ready to be shown by whomever is inside at the time. Some agents post signs that specifically instruct, DO NOT DISTURB OCCUPANTS. You might consider this.

If you are selling your home without an agent it is still important to act as professionally as possible. This means having a professionally created sign—no homemade ones. Most signmakers, listed in the local Yellow Pages, have standard

signs to which they need only add your phone number. Or you can get something at a local hardware store for a few dollars.

❏ *Bulletin Boards.* These can be found just about anywhere people congregate: grocery stores, schools, public libraries, places of worship, community centers, laundromats, and offices. This type of notice need not be as slick as your front-yard sign. You can scrawl something on a sheet of paper, if you must, although it will be better if neatly typed. To grab attention, you might paste a flattering color photo of the property in the middle of the sheet. (You can bring a negative to a local photo processing outlet and get 4" x 5" reprints for about thirty cents each.) Again, if you include your phone number, specify the hours during which you'll accept calls.

❏ *Television.* This is no joke. Many real estate agencies are now running half-hour programs—what in effect are long commercials—to sell homes on local cable and broadcast stations. A typical show features thirty to sixty homes, "taking you inside each home," as the producers like to say, so you can get a more or less firsthand look at these prospective properties.

PHONE AND GAMES

When your ad does appear, you'll receive anywhere from a few to a lot of calls. It is important that a principal owner of the house field the calls. Don't rely on a child, elderly parent, uninformed spouse, or other surrogate salesperson to take calls. Many callers will be pursuing several ads at once, and if they can't get the information they need right off the bat, they may simply move on to the next prospect. If you must leave someone else in charge, by no means should you have that individual discuss price or other important details on the phone. His or her sole responsibility is to take down the names and phone numbers of all callers.

When you talk with callers, your two principal goals will be to determine whether they are bona fide prospects and get them to come see your house if they are. First determine whether a caller is truly interested in inspecting your home for possible purchase (as opposed to casing the joint as a potential burglary target) and whether they are financially capable of pull the deal off should they like what they see. It is to your advantage to get

to know your callers as quickly as possible. Are they first-time buyers? If so, they will be nervous, possibly stressed, about the home-search process, requiring that you engage in a bit more hand-holding than with more seasoned buyers. You might want to find out how many homes they already looked at. If this is the first, you can assume that they'll be looking at plenty of others before making a decision; if it's their fifteenth house, they'll be looking for something new and different. Is the caller buying for himself or herself, or looking for an investment? An investor will be much more interested in the money side of things, as opposed to the owner-resident, who will be equally interested in the features of the house that make it livable.

Speaking of money, you'll save considerable time by qualifying callers before they come over. Find out whether they've lined up financing, or whether they presently own their home (if they do, they'll likely have some equity to put down on a new home, and will generally have an easier time getting a mortgage). There's no reason why you can't ask them what they do for a living and how much they make.

For your part, don't talk price over the phone. Stick to the qualities of the house itself. You're not negotiating yet, you're only trying to get them to come inspect the merchandise. If they're persistent with their questions, tell them, "You really must come see it." If they're really interested, arrange a specific day and time. Don't accept vague commitments such as "I'll stop by sometime this weekend." This will tie up your Saturday (or whenever) as you wait for someone who may or may not show up. Ask the individual's name and number before hanging up. Some callers may be reluctant to give this out, but if something comes up, you'll be glad you had a way to get in touch.

Sometimes an enthusiastic caller wants to see your home right away. Stories are legion of couples who heard about buyers falling in love with a property and making an offer on the spot. For example, a couple hears about (or drives by) an available property on Saturday night and calls the agent (or owner) at home immediately. The agent (or owner) shows the house first thing Sunday morning and by dinnertime there's a deal on the table, perhaps even accepted. So unless there are compelling reasons to do so, don't discourage the caller who wants instant access to your house. Forget that the house is a total mess. The prospective buyer will have to see through the chaos.

THE FACT SHEET

Either you or your agent should put together a one-page property description of your property, listing pertinent facts about your house:

- ❏ number of bedrooms
- ❏ number of bathrooms
- ❏ the house's age
- ❏ descriptions, including sizes, of other rooms
- ❏ descriptions of kitchen appliances
- ❏ descriptions of other appliances
- ❏ descriptions of house structure and systems
- ❏ square footage of living space and yard
- ❏ cost of utilities and taxes
- ❏ zoning restrictions
- ❏ location of public transportation, schools, and shopping
- ❏ other special features
- ❏ price
- ❏ your (or your agent's) name, address, and phone number

You might also want to include a drawing of the floor plan for each floor and, perhaps, a photograph of the house itself. The sheet should be neatly typed, with enough photocopies available for anyone who asks. (You might also hand these out to your friends and colleagues, who may know someone who happens to be in the market for a house. This sheet could also double as your bulletin board ad.)

The more you include on this sheet, the better. Don't assume that anything is obvious. Assume instead that the reader will return from a day of marathon home inspecting and will have only your sheet to remember the specific attributes of your property. And assume that the person will read it again in a few days when the memory of your house has grown even dimmer.

A sample fact sheet is included on the next page.

GETTING YOUR PAPERS IN ORDER

The fact sheet is only the beginning. To be an effective salesperson, you should pull together a neatly organized packet of other documents, for inspection by anyone who asks. While it's pos-

```
+--------------------------------+
|                                |
|         Photo Here             |
|         (optional)             |
|                                |
+--------------------------------+
```

3303 Porter Street
Anytown, Minnesota

2,450 square feet	Smoke detectors throughout
.76 acre lot	Forced-air heat (gas furnace)
4 bedrooms	Thermal windows
2$\frac{1}{2}$ bath	Double-wall construction
Modern kitchen (built-in range)	Cedar shake roof
Dishwasher	1,275-square-foot backyard w/
Disposal	swing set
Wall-to-wall carpet downstairs	Easy-to-care front lawn
Fireplace	.4 miles to shopping
Dining room	.6 miles to elementary school
Family room	taxes last year: $825
Washer/dryer (4 years old)	Utilities last year: $1,470
100-amp electrical service	Zoned R-2
1-car garage plus driveway	Built 1973

$98,500

Terms: Prefer all-cash, but will consider small second mortgage to assumable balance of $39,500. Will pay half of all closing costs for all-cash sale.

Contact:
Mary or Al Jones
555-1234

sible that no one will ask, if someone does, you'll be ready with an impressive array of information. The packet should include:

❑ Your deed or title to the property
❑ Your first (and second) mortgage papers
❑ Your property tax bills for the past year
❑ Your utility bills for the past year
❑ A property survey, showing the size of the property and its boundaries
❑ An inspection report, if you have one
❑ An appraisal report, if you have one
❑ Lists of receipts for major improvements and repairs you've made

SOME LAST-MINUTE TOUCHES

Before you let the teaming masses in to inspect your property, there are a few important last-minute touches you should consider.

❑ *Let the sun shine in.* Make the house look as light and airy as possible. You want to make a bright, cheery impression. If it's winter, light a fire in the fireplace. If it's summer, make sure the house is well air-conditioned.

❑ *Bake something.* This is a classic, but it still works. There's nothing that will give your house a good better feeling than the smell of a freshly baked pie, cookies, or bread. Other ways to make your house smell nice (*subtly*, please—you don't want to bowl over prospective buyers with overwhelming aromas) are to dab some scented oils on a bathroom towel or to place a fresh bouquet of flowers on the dining room table. Still another technique is to turn on your electric stove to a low setting and sprinkle a little cinnamon or clover over it.

❑ *Turn on some music.* A little light music wouldn't hurt either. Turn on the stereo to something soft and a little bland—no Twisted Sister or Stravinsky. It will help create a relaxed mood. And keep the TV off.

❑ *Get rid of the kids.* The fewer people in the house at the time you're showing it, the better. That's especially true for four-

legged creatures; however cute they may be, a lot of people don't like pets or are allergic to them.

❏ *Have a guest book.* By having visitors sign in with their names and phone numbers, you'll not only act professionally, you'll have a ready list of prospects with whom you can check back in a few days. A good salesperson always follows up.

SHOWING IT OFF

OK, it's show time. Your house has never looked better and you—with or without an agent—are ready to have an open house, whether a formal one (advertised in the newspaper classifieds and on bulletin boards, stating a specific day and time) or an informal one (you've invited a few callers to drop by on a specific day and and at a specific time, but have not opened it up to the home-buying public). Here are some tips to get the best results from your efforts:

❏ When they arrive, introduce yourself to your visitors, give them the fact sheet, and ask them to sign in. Tell them you will be available to answer questions.

❏ Then *leave them alone.* Don't hover around, commenting on everything they see. If they have questions, they'll ask. Most people want to make their own inspections, at their own pace. But don't be afraid to point out things they might otherwise miss.

❏ Don't act overanxious. There's nothing that will put off a prospective buyer more than someone who won't let things happen naturally, in a relaxed manner.

You'll begin to learn pretty quickly that some of the visitors are serious potential buyers while others are merely "tourists." And some of the buyers will be able to afford your house, while others won't. (Don't let appearances fool you. Even that best-dressed couple in the Mercedes could be so full of debt that they'd never qualify for a mortgage.)

Of course, you should treat everyone with equal respect, as if any one of them could suddenly materialize with an attractive offer. At the same time, you should watch out for the tire-kickers, those less-than-serious shoppers who will drain you of your

precious time and raise your expectations falsely. The fact is, there are quite a lot of people who like to drop in on open houses as a sort of hobby, whether to pick up a few home-decorating ideas or merely for the vicarious pleasures of seeing how other people live.

WHAT TO SAY, WHAT NOT TO SAY

Everyone's different, and everyone looks at homes differently. Some people want to be left alone, others want to be accompanied. Some people like to go through the process in silence, others like to talk their way through it. To be a good salesperson when you show your home, you'll have to evaluate each prospective buyer, and treat him or her accordingly.

There's a good case to be made that the less you say, the better. Some shy types find themselves overwhelmed by enthusiastic, talkative sellers; they may want to get away from such an uncomfortable situation as quickly as possible. Those less-than-shy types—the ones who need to run their mouths, commenting on everything they see—are likely to do their own selling: If they like something, they'll talk themselves into it; if they don't they'll talk themselves out of it. Better to accommodate both types by simply being available to answer questions. Silence, in this case, may well be golden.

In any case, when you do answer questions, don't just give factual answers. People aren't just buying a house; they're buying an entire lifestyle. When you talk about your kitchen, don't merely describe its features, however numerous they may be. Talk instead about how your family used it comfortably, and how nice Sunday morning breakfast was with everyone hanging around the kitchen for hours. Of course, don't be overly dramatic, either. People will see through that immediately.

Don't apologize for things you don't like about your home. Everyone has several such items; they might, in fact, be the reasons you are selling it in the first place. While honesty should always be your policy when selling your home, there is no reason to give an otherwise good property a bad rap. Just the facts. If there are obvious defects, by all means make them known, lest you be accused of covering up and misrepresenting your house. But to point out that "I never liked the bedroom; it's the darkest room in the house" will get you nowhere.

Some viewers will offer seemingly disparaging comments—

"I really was hoping for a bigger living room," or "I'm not sure whether there's enough storage space for all my junk." That doesn't mean the individual doesn't like your house, or won't eventually make you an offer. It's simply the process some people go through out loud to imagine themselves living there. In fact, such criticisms might be a good sign. They could indicate that someone is seriously considering buying. You might have more reason to be concerned if someone just says, "Gee, what a nice house."

In general, be accommodating to prospective buyers. If they want to come back two, three, or four times, by all means let them do so. Some shoppers need such multiple visits to make a decision. Sometimes they also bring with them friends, parents, lawyers, architects, or whomever—or they may simply come by themselves to wander through aimlessly, imagining what life would be like living there.

If you have listed your home with a real estate agent, he or she will serve as your surrogate, dealing directly with many of these shoppers. But that shouldn't give you license to excuse yourself from the process entirely. Unless something prohibits you from doing so—not the least of which is the fact that you've already moved and are safely ensconced in your new abode—you should be an active participant in the process. No one knows your home better than you do, and no one else can sell its features and charm. Your active participation will increase the likelihood that you'll get an offer sooner rather than later.

Now, let's get down to some wheeling and dealing.

Chapter 5
Wheeling and Dealing

You can use all the help you can get when it comes time to wheel and deal on your house. This is no task for the fainthearted. We're talking about tens of thousands of dollars—perhaps a hundred thousand or more. Having some good help on hand may save you far more than it will cost in professional fees.

Remember that if you are being represented by a real estate agent, he or she will be your principal ally. The agent is being paid a commission by you, so there is an incentive built in: The higher the sales price, the more money the agent will receive.

If you're selling on your own, consider hiring a lawyer. You may shudder at the mere thought of engaging such a professional—lawyers don't, after all, have the highest level of our society's trust—but it may well be worth the few hundred dollars it will cost you. Most lawyers are adept at sorting through the seemingly endless array of fine-print forms you must go through when selling real estate. Most are also skilled negotiators, something at which most of us lay people aren't particularly good. And the same attorney who will help you through negotiations can also hold your hand through closing.

As with finding a lender, your search for a lawyer may begin with a bank, friends, your employer, or the local bar association. When you first call the lawyer to make an appointment, there are several things you should ask:

❏ What services will you provide, and at what fee (ideally broken down by service)?
❏ What experience do you have in real estate?
❏ Will you negotiate with the buyer on my behalf?
❏ Will you attend the closing?

CONSIDERING AN OFFER

Conventional wisdom has it that sellers always ask more for their property than they expect to get, so that there is always room to lower the price. As with most conventional wisdom, it

often isn't true. A significant number of sellers *know* what their home is worth and list it at that price, including the word "firm." A buyer can either pay it or look elsewhere. And many homes truly are excellent buys at their full asking prices. So don't assume that your selling price *must* eventually be lowered. You may be able to stand your ground and get your price.

"Firm" prices are particularly common during a seller's market, in which there are more buyers than sellers, and in certain real estate markets or particularly desirable neighborhoods, where affordable housing is at a premium. In some areas, in fact, housing prices often sell *above* their asking price, as two or more would-be buyers bid each other up. Clearly, for these buyers, the specific house or location is more important than getting the lowest price.

But there are other considerations beyond price that can make the sales terms more favorable to you; more about those in a moment.

The offer to buy is a formal process with specific rules that must be followed. It is not like haggling over a used car, in which two parties sit in the seller's living room or talk on the phone and casually make offers and counteroffers. In real estate, the offer—usually known as an offer to purchase or a sales agreement—is made in writing. It is a formal document, signed and dated, and is a legally binding contract that states how much the buyer will pay for the house, provided certain conditions are met.

The offer will have a time limit—a couple of days in which you must either accept or reject it. You may always ask for more time, but buyers likely will think twice about granting it unless there is good reason to do so. It is to your advantage to have as much time as possible; if there are other interested buyers, additional time will allow you to "shop" the offer around, perhaps getting a second offer at a higher price. In the ideal world, that could lead to a bidding war. For example, you might say to the other interested party, "I've been offered $75,000. If you make it $78,000, it's yours." The first buyer might insist on having the right to top any other offer the seller receives, assuming it makes sense to do so. Fine, let them have it.

If you are working with an agent, he or she will accept the offer on your behalf. Keep in mind that the buyer can revoke the offer at any time until you accept it. If you reject the offer, you cannot later accept it unless it is rewritten and formally resub-

mitted by the buyer. When the buyer signs the offer, he or she must also put down some "earnest money," indicating that the buyer is serious about all this. The amount varies, usually under $1,000, perhaps pegged at 1 percent of the sale price. The money will be placed in escrow, to be applied toward the purchase price at settlement, or returned to the buyer if the deal falls through.

In addition to accepting or rejecting the offer, you have a third option: a counteroffer. The buyer, then, can accept, reject, or counter your counteroffer, with offers going back and forth until there is a resolution either way. All of this happens fairly rapidly, usually in a few days. Usually, too, both you and the buyer are anxious for things to resolve—you don't want the buyer to have a change of heart; the buyer wants to know whether or not to keep looking—so it isn't in anyone's interest to sit on an offer or counteroffer for very long. It's important to keep things on a pleasant and reasonable level, because even after both parties accept the offer, there's still plenty to negotiate.

When you decide to accept an offer, the next step is to execute a purchase agreement, which must be done within a certain number of days, according to state law. It is in the purchase agreement that you will negotiate a lot of additional terms and conditions associated with the sale.

Negotiating price is a delicate matter. There are no rules of thumb for how much a buyer will offer below the sales price, although it is extremely rare that a house sells for 20 percent or more less than your asking price. Just like your asking price, the buyer's opening offer is derived from calculations that could be described as more art than science, and a great deal of its success depends on plain old luck. For example, if no one else is bidding on a property and you are anxious to sell it, or if someone who outbids the first buyer is unable to secure financing or meet other conditions, you might accept a low offer if you are in a hurry to sell. Obviously, your particular needs will play a major role.

Deciding to accept an offer depends on a number of things that only you can determine. Deciding that an offered price is acceptable will involve both logic and emotion, as well as your particular needs. It may be that you must sell it fast, and will accept the first offer within reason. It may be that there are no other offers. Or you may want to hang in there and wait for someone to come closer to your asking price.

Of course, the same goes for the buyer. He or she may need

to find a place immediately (perhaps they've already sold their present home and must move out by a fixed date) and will be willing to pay a little bit more than they might otherwise pay to ensure that you'll accept the offer. Or, they may have a fixed amount in mind, and won't budge a penny over it. Having a professional on your side will help reduce the second guessing, and will increase the chances you'll get the best possible offer.

By the way, don't take your property off the market once you've received an offer. In real estate, offers fall through all the time, even after you've agreed on price. Only after all contingencies of a contract have been removed should you stop accepting offers. You may accept a second offer as a "back-up" offer, which binds you to accept the second offer if the first one falls through. But the back-up contract must state clearly that it is a back-up contract and will not become binding until you notify the buyer in writing that the offer has been accepted.

THE PURCHASE AGREEMENT

Price negotiations were the easy part: There was only one matter to agree on. Now it's time to negotiate the terms of sale, including a host of details you probably haven't thought much about. Among other details, the purchase agreement will state:

❑ the price of the property
❑ what's included in the sale (house, land, fixtures, appliances, etc.)
❑ the date of sale (the "closing") and when the buyer can move in
❑ the contingencies—under what conditions you or the buyer can get out of the agreement

Purchase agreements vary widely from city to city and state to state, so having an agent or lawyer will be helpful. Keep in mind that everything is negotiable, and even if something is neatly printed on a standard form, it may still be changed, as long as both parties agree to the change and initial the modifications.

Let's examine the key components of the basic purchase agreement.

❑ *Earnest money*. When you sign the purchase agreement, the buyer will be required to make a deposit on the house. This is

called earnest money. It is a token cash amount—usually $500 to $1,000—that binds you and the buyer to the terms of the agreement. In some cases, deposits can be for as little as $100. The money will be held by the broker, your lawyer, or some other third party. While this money is refundable if the deal doesn't go through, it is in your interest to obtain as much as possible in earnest money; in general, the more money one puts down, the more commitment it represents. Right now, you're looking for as much commitment as possible.

❑ *Price and terms.* The purchase agreement will state the price, and whether it will be an all cash deal—that is, paid in full at the time of closing—or whether there will be any other financing arrangements.

❑ *The particulars.* This includes a legal description of the property, the expiration date of the offer, and the date of closing and occupancy.

❑ *Contingencies.* These can be many and varied, depending on any unique aspects of the deal. The following are the most common:

1. A *financing contingency* indicates that the contract depends on the buyer's ability to obtain a mortgage or other financing within a given period of time—say, thirty to forty-five days—and at a stated interest rate and length of term. Such a clause might read: "This purchase offer is contingent upon buyer and the property qualifying within thirty days for a new first mortgage of at least $60,000 at a fixed interest rate not exceeding 10.5 percent for a term of thirty years and a loan fee not exceeding two points." So, if the buyer can't get the money at the terms he or she wants, the deal's off and you must refund the deposit.

2. *Inspection contingencies* indicate that the deal hinges on the buyer having inspections done on the house to his or her satisfaction for such things as termites and other pests, radon, the electrical system, plumbing, the structure, and the appliances. The contingency must state the time period within which the inspections must be completed. The

contingency may state that the contract will become null and void if the inspections reveal certain conditions, such as termites, unsafe aluminum wiring, asbestos insulation, or other potential hazards or defects. Or, these problems could result in credits from you to the buyer toward the purchase price, roughly equivalent to the amount it would take to remedy the problems, or the approximate value they detract from the property. Remember: *everything's negotiable.*

3. An *appraisal contingency* states that the offer may be withdrawn if the house is not appraised for at least a specific amount. This may be particularly important in the buyer getting a VA- or FHA-insured loan.

4. *Sale of buyer's house contingency* states that if the buyer is unable to sell his or her existing home within a given time period, the purchase agreement becomes null and void.

❑ *Agreement of condition.* This will ensure that the property on which the buyer makes an offer is the same property he or she will get, and that there are no hidden defects that you haven't disclosed. For example: "Seller represents that all defects in this property known to the seller have been disclosed to the buyer in writing." The buyer will likely ask that the offer is contingent "upon buyer obtaining a satisfactory inspection report on the property from a professional property inspector of buyer's choice at buyer's expense within five business days." If the buyer insists on a clause stating that the property will be in the same condition as it is on the date of the offer, ordinary and reasonable wear and tear notwithstanding, you might consider protecting yourself by asking your insurance agent for a binder on the property during this period; your existing homeowner's policy may already cover this.

❑ *Completion of work.* If any work is being done on the house by you, the contract may indicate that the work must be completed prior to settlement.

❑ *What's included in the sale.* The contract should include an inventory of items that both you and the buyer agree are part of

the deal. Aside from the house itself, these items may include appliances, lighting fixtures, carpets, mirrors, patio furniture, tools, supplies, and anything else that isn't physically attached to the house.

❑ *Vacate or rent.* If you don't move out of the house in time for the buyer to take possession, you may have to agree to pay the buyer's living expenses for the period in which he or she must find other arrangements. Alternatively, upon settlement you could become a tenant in the buyer's new house and pay rent during your stay. If either of these conditions is appropriate, it should be stated in the purchase agreement.

❑ *Taxes and utilities.* Property tax bills arrive once or twice a year, so it's possible that you will have prepaid some of the property taxes for the period following settlement. If so, you should stipulate that you will be reimbursed by the buyer at settlement for the prepaid taxes. The same may be true for utilities: If you recently filled an oil or propane tank, and that fuel will convey to the buyer, the buyer may have to pay for it.

❑ *Title.* "Title" in real estate refers to legal ownership, the way it is recorded in public records. When people borrow money and puts up their home for collateral, that is usually recorded on the official title. Other legal proceedings, from contracts to bankruptcies to lawsuits, also can place a cloud on the title. The title records are the final determinant of property ownership, and it is vital that the title to a house you are selling be free and clear.

In the purchase agreement, you must "warrant"—that is, promise or prove—that you will deliver at settlement a "marketable" title, one that is free and clear of all liens and encumbrances except those which you and the buyer specifically agree to in the contract or approve when the results of the title search are completed. You may negotiate as to who will pay for the title search service to determine whether the title is clear. Before a property transfer can legally take place, a title search must be conducted to determine that the seller has the legal right to transfer title to a new owner.

❑ *Closing costs.* Usually the buyer pays most of these costs—loan charges and title insurance, for example. However, once again,

everything is negotiable, and the buyer's broker or lawyer may try to save them some money by asking you to share some of these costs.

❑ *Buyer default*. You should add a buyer default clause, stating that if the buyer backs out of the deal for reasons other than stated in this purchase agreement, you may keep the deposit. If you'd like, you could go so far as to sue the buyer for damages, up to and including the full purchase price of the house. The buyer, in turn, may seek a *seller's default* clause, stating that if you change your mind and back out of the sale, you must pay the buyer an amount equal to or even double the amount of your deposit.

❑ *Arbitration clause*. Sometimes, problems arise before, during, or after settlement that can't be easily negotiated between the buyer and seller, and for which neither party wants to file an expensive and time-consuming lawsuit. One common alternative is to provide for binding arbitration by the American Arbitration Association, which provides skilled arbitrators to help work out equitable solutions; because it is binding, you are agreeing to abide by the outcome of the arbitration. The clause probably should state that the buyer and seller will share equally the cost of the arbitration, which may run to several hundred dollars.

❑ *Signatures*. Make sure that all buyers—a husband and wife or parent, among others, if the title to the house is to be jointly held—sign the document.

Look over the purchase agreement carefully. It plots the course for all that is to follow in the home-selling process, and a few key phrases—whether included or omitted—can make all the difference. Keep in mind that there are many points of negotiation involved with the purchase agreement, the results of which can cost or save you hundreds or thousands of dollars. Don't sign the purchase agreement until both you and the buyer agree on all the terms.

MONEY TALKS

Why should you be concerned about financing when you're

selling? Isn't that the buyer's responsibility?

Yes and no. Yes, it is the buyer who must come up with the money to buy your house. But if the buyer—like many buyers—isn't easily able to come up with the tens of thousands of dollars needed, you the seller will have to help out.

Chances are that you won't come across someone with $75,000 or so burning a hole in his or her pocket, ready, willing, and able to hand it over to you for the title to your house. Nearly everyone who buys a house must finance it, and their ability to obtain financing in a reasonable amount of time is directly related to your need to unload your house within some time limit.

On top of that, as seller, you have the right to know something about the finances of whomever is interested in your house. Can they really afford it—not just the down payment, but also the monthly payments? If not, is it worth it for you to help them in some way? Obviously, you won't be doing this for nothing. You will somehow be compensated for your trouble—a higher sales price, for example, or a loan that pays you a monthly fee for anywhere from a few months to a few years. (Of course, one other benefit to you for helping with financing may be that it is the only way to sell your home. If your home has problems, or if you're selling in a buyer's market, such incentives may be necessary for you to find a buyer. If so, that ability to sell may be compensation enough.)

So, there are two key aspects of home-buying finances with which you the seller must be concerned: qualifying prospective buyers, and ensuring their ability to finance the purchase.

SELLER FINANCING

It's increasingly common that the seller participate in the financing. Of course, there must be something in it for you to do so; sometimes that something is simply making it easier to sell your house. If you are having trouble finding a buyer, or if market conditions just aren't right for selling, these "creative financing" techniques may work like a dream. For example, you can:

❏ defer part of the down payment for a few years
❏ lend the buyer the money for the down payment as a balloon loan, in which the buyer pays only the interest portion for, say, five years, at which time the principal comes due in a lump sum

(another advantage is that it may qualify the buyer for an 80 percent mortgage, one that is easier to obtain)
❑ have the buyer assume your present mortgage, if it's assumable
❑ rent your house with an option to buy it later, with some of the rent going toward a down payment

Here are the basic types of seller-financing arrangements to consider:

❑ *Loan assumption.* One of the easiest solutions is for the buyer to assume your loan. Most loans made before 1980 and some loans made since then are assumable—their terms may be taken over by someone other than the loan applicant, including the buyer of the property. And many of those assumable loans are extremely attractive—5 or 6 percent, for example. On the other hand, if you have owned the house a while, you likely have built up considerable equity, which the buyer will have to cover in the form of a substantial down payment. For example, your house is selling for $80,000, for which you have a $35,000 mortgage balance at 6 percent interest. To assume the loan, the buyer will have to come up with $45,000 in cash to pay you off. It may be possible to take out a second mortgage for that amount at current interest rates. The difference in monthly payments of the two loans—the 6 percent loan and the current-market-rate one—should be significantly below what the buyer would pay if he or she got a mortgage for the full amount at current rates. Of course, you, realizing that the assumable mortgage is worth something, will likely want to be compensated for the low-interest gift—probably in the form of a higher selling price. You should be aware that laws governing assumable loans vary from state to state.

❑ *Second mortgage.* Second mortgages are available from a variety of sources, and you may be as good a source as any. The second, which most likely will be used to supplement the down payment when the buyer obtains a principal mortgage, can be arranged in a variety of ways. Most advantageous to the buyer, particularly during the first few years of owning a home, is for the loan to be spread out over, say, five years, paying interest only every month, with a balloon payment due after five years

(although it could be repayable as short as one year later, or as long as ten). Presumably, after that time, the buyer will be on more stable financial ground, or the house will have appreciated sufficiently that he or she could refinance it and pay off the second mortgage. There are variations even on this theme, such as amortizing the five-year loan over a thirty-year period, meaning that the buyer's monthly payments would be the same size as if he or she had taken a thirty-year loan; then, in effect, the buyer prepays the loan after five years. The possibilities are many and varied.

❑ *Take-back mortgage.* This is a confusing term describing an arrangement in which you provide all of the financing (except the down payment), possibly in combination with an assumable mortgage. With you as lender, the buyer can be somewhat more creative in putting together a financial package than he or she could be with most financial institutions. Let's say, for example, the purchase price is $100,000. The buyer could put down 10 percent, assume your $35,000 mortgage, and have you take back the balance of $55,000 in a five-year interest-only note. After five years, the buyer will face a hefty balloon payment, but he or she will probably be in a much better position to refinance the property, which by then may well be worth $135,000 or more. If your mortgage isn't assumable, you still could take back the entire mortgage, part of which could be in the form of a balloon, part of which could be a standard mortgage. Needless to say, you'll need an accountant and a lawyer to create the optimal scenario for both parties.

❑ *Wraparound mortgage.* If your mortgage isn't assumable, one good arrangement is the wraparound. Let's say the buyer is paying $100,000 on the house, for which you have a $35,000 mortgage. You would take back all the financing but would keep paying off your original mortgage, presumably one with an attractive low-interest rate. Let's say the buyer puts down 20 percent and assumes monthly payments of about $800 a month for the $80,000 mortgage. You take that $800 and make monthly payments of $300 on your original mortgage and keep the remaining $500. In effect, the buyer has "wrapped" a mortgage around yours. But keep in mind that your lender may not approve of this arrangement; if the original mortgage has a "due

on sale" clause, you'll be required to pay off the original mortgage when title of the house is transferred to the buyer.

❑ *Rent with the option to buy*. This is a novel arrangement that can work well for both parties. In a rent-with-option arrangement, the buyer rents the property from you with the right to purchase it at a specific price within a specific time period. In the typical arrangement, part of your rent would be applied to the down payment. This situation works best during a time of high interest rates, allowing the buyer to buy time until rates come back down to a reasonable level, or when you want to temporarily forego income to delay or avoid capital gains taxes. There's some risk, of course, that time will run out on the buyer's rental period and he or she still won't have adequate or reasonable financing. It also keeps your options open.

All seller-financing arrangements require some careful planning, as well as good legal and financial advice. Carefully and thoughtfully executed, however, seller financing can provide the best possible arrangement for both buyer and seller.

One important word of caution: Be extremely wary of any arrangement in which the buyer does not put down any money. There are thousands of no-money-down hustlers out there—some legit, some not so legit—who thrive on making killings in the real estate market without using any of their own money. In most cases, these are investors: They will buy the house and rent it out for enough money to pay the mortgage. But even with the owner occupying the house, no-money-down deals offer very little incentive for the buyer to make payments as promised. If you've financed all or part of the deal—playing banker, in effect—you may be caught holding the bag. You'll have to sue to recover your property, which is a very expensive proposition, perhaps while continuing to make payments to *your* lender. Tread cautiously, and make sure you get legal counsel.

IF YOUR HOUSE ISN'T SELLING

Sometimes, things simply don't work out as planned. Whether it's the house, the neighborhood, interest rates, or the local real estate market, some houses take months and months to sell.

What can you do? Well, lowering the sales price is one obvious tactic; it could bring buyers running. Another step is to

take the house off the market for a few weeks. After appearing in classified ads or multiple listings for weeks on end, a house can get a reputation as a "tired" property. Agents will be reluctant to show it, simply because it's been on the market for so long—there *must* be something wrong with it.

Consider carefully the options listed above. Have you made your house as attractive to buy as possible? Are there things you could do to improve its appearance? Are there financing techniques you haven't considered that might make the deal more attractive?

Listen carefully to disparaging comments prospective buyers have made about your house. Is it the house? Its condition? The neighborhood? However hard it may be to hear these things, it's better to know than not know.

A last resort, of course, is to rent it out. If you've owned your house for more than a couple of years, it's likely that rents are high enough—and your mortgage payments low enough—that the rent you would receive would cover your mortgage and other costs. And, of course, you'll continue to get attractive mortgage-interest deductions, among other tax breaks. True, you'll become a landlord, with all its inherent responsibilities and headaches. But it's better than nothing, and you might even find it to be a profitable venture.

In a few months or a year, you can put your house on the market again, perhaps with more favorable results. Meanwhile, let's move on to the final step: closing.

Chapter 6
Signing, Sealing, Delivering

This is the day it all happens: The buyer pays his or her money, you both sign the papers, and the house is no longer yours. However simple that may sound, settlement (also known as closing) can be a complicated, time-consuming process, and it should be approached as seriously as any other aspect of selling a home.

Settlement practices vary from locality to locality, and even within the same county or city. Depending on location, settlements may be conducted by lending institutions, title-insurance companies, escrow companies, real estate brokers, and attorneys for either the buyer or seller. Needless to say, whoever conducts settlement will be paid handsomely for the effort, although the amount will vary widely; the buyer will pay most of this. However, you should be represented, either by your real estate agent or by an attorney experienced in real estate closings.

GOING TO SETTLEMENT
Depending upon the state or city in which it takes place, settlement may seem kind of like the final scene in a mystery movie, in which everyone you've seen throughout the film shows up at the same time in one room. There may be you, the seller (if more than one person owns the property—even a husband and wife—both parties should attend); the buyer (similarly, if there is more than one person buying both parties should attend); lawyers for both parties; the real estate agent; a representative of the lender; a representative of the title insurance company; and probably a notary public for good luck.

To make sure that everything goes according to plan at settlement, there are a few things you should bring with you to settlement:

❏ your title policy
❏ the names of all parties who have an interest in the property,

such as lenders, trust deed holders, and any other liens or encumbrances
❑ your current tax receipts or bills
❑ a set of keys to the house

If you have an agent, he or she will have a handy checklist to remind you of all these—and probably a few other—things. You should check regularly with the agent and buyer beginning a week or so before the scheduled closing date to make sure that all papers are in order. With the seemingly endless details involved, you'd be surprised how many pieces of paper seem to get lost in the shuffle.

Closing will be held in the offices of an attorney, lender, or the title insurance company. You will sit around a big table and sign lots of things. It's an endless parade of paper, all of which should be read by you and your lawyer or other representative. Inevitably, there will be something missing, a state of affairs that may take anywhere from a few minutes to a few days to rectify.

There may be some last-minute haggling at settlement, perhaps regarding things you did not leave in the house that the buyer expected to be there; or perhaps you left a lot of junk around after you moved, and the buyer had to pay to have it removed. Meanwhile, you may want to seek reimbursement for anything you've prepaid—taxes, utilities, and insurance. With luck, all these items will have been planned for and taken care of in the purchase agreement signed earlier. But, as you well know, such luck isn't always on your side.

When all the paper-shuffling and check-writing has been finished, the deal will be done. If you have a mortgage that you will be paying off on settlement, the title company will likely pay the lender directly. The only thing that's left is for you to receive your net profit—the difference between the sales price less any reductions, the balance on your existing mortgage, and any commissions due real estate agents. The rest of the money is yours.

Congratulations! You have just successfully sold your house!